EARLY PIETY

EARLY PIETY

a CALL to the RISING GENERATION

Edited by Scott Brown

NCFIC

WAKE FOREST, NORTH CAROLINA

A Course Of Sermons On Early Piety

By the Eight Ministers
Who Carry On The Thursday Lecture In Boston.

With a Preface and Closing
by the Reverend Dr. Increase Mather.

Hac Casti Maneant in Religione Nepotes.

Boston: In N.E.

Printed by S. Kneeland
for N. Buttolph, B. Eliot, and D. Henchman
and Sold at Their Shops. 1721.

First Printing: January 2016

Copyright © 2016 The National Center for Family-Integrated Churches
All Rights Reserved

The National Center for Family-Integrated Churches
220 South White St., Wake Forest, NC 27587
www.ncfic.org

ISBN-10: 1-62418-057-4
ISBN-13: 978-1-62418-057-6

Book Design and Typography by Justin Turley and Colton Neifert

Scripture references in this book are taken from the King James Version, originally published 1611. Used by permission. All rights reserved.

Printed in the United States of America.

OTHER BOOKS *from the* NCFIC

A Theology of the Family

A Weed in the Church

Counterfeit Worship

Family Reformation

Feminine by Design

It Can Be Done

Moment of Courage

Preparing Boys for Battle

Preparing for Marriage

ACKNOWLEDGEMENTS

I would like to thank the many people who helped me with this volume. First, my gratitude must first be expressed for Dan Ford and Jim Zes who so kindly introduced me to a first edition of this volume. I'll always be grateful for the day I read that old leather bound book from 1721. When I finished it, I felt it should be published in a modern format. That was over ten years ago.

Editing books from the 18th century is often a challenge. It is difficult to strike the balance between preserving the original language and updating it enough for readability. For this part of the task, I especially want to thank Jonathan Sides, Jonathan Tanaka, The Harris family, Deborah Brown, Claudia Brown, David Brown, John Ward, Michael Tutor, Parker Stearns, Connor Stearns, Colton Neifert. All of these labored diligently in typing, editing, proofreading and research.

ENDORSEMENTS

"I highly recommended Early Piety as a book that meets one of the greatest needs of our day. It is a voice calling to young people in the wilderness of this world to live and walk soli Deo gloria!. And, it is a valuable tool for parents to teach us how to pray for and train our children. May God use this excellent book to instill true piety or godliness early in the lives of many.

–Dr. Joel R. Beeke, President, Puritan Reformed Theological Seminary, Grand Rapids, Michigan

"These sermons are unique in that they not only provide careful instruction in the gospel, but also, in the godliness or true piety that springs forth from it. If these sermons are read thoughtfully by parents and older youth, if they are explained carefully and diligently to younger children, then they are bound to bear an abundant harvest. Such a blend of gospel, wisdom, and piety is very rare."

—Paul Washer, Director of HeartCry Missionary Society

INTRODUCTION
For Young People Raised in Christian Homes

This book was written for young people raised in Christian homes. It contains some of the most beautiful, penetrating appeals I have ever read. The authors wrestle with souls. They call readers to, examine themselves to see if they are in the faith (2 Cor. 13:5). It is a book to help you know who you are; what kingdom you serve; your eternal destiny. It is a tool for personal examination.

How did it originate? It was a series of sermons that pastors in Boston preached in 1721, during the ministry of Increase Mather and his son Cotton. At the time of writing, Increase was at the end of his life at age 83, and his son Cotton was 58.

The pastors in Boston were very concerned about the loss of godliness in the rising generation. Children who were raised up in the training and admonition of the Lord were straying. To meet this critical moment in the history of New England, they gathered together in Boston to address the youth directly. They met for Thursday afternoon lectures where whole families listened to preaching directed to the youth and parents.

When I first read this book, I was astonished at the insight these pastors had into the hearts of youth raised in Christian homes. I felt that it would be a wonderful resource for families to read out loud together. I am confident that doing so would achieve much good in families who name the name of Christ. The gospel is clearly proclaimed and the doctrine of regeneration is explained. It is an excellent tool for young people to examine their souls.

I pray that young people reading this book would find themselves saying things like, "now, It is clear – I know I am a child of God." Or, I thought I was converted, but now I know I am not. Perhaps some would find themselves like the prodigal son, where it was said, "he came to his senses" (Luke 15:17).

I pray that young people raised in Christian homes would read this book and be assured of their salvation or be disturbed out of their sleep.

Scott T. Brown

a **PREFACE** *by* **DR. INCREASE MATHER**

When these eight ministers agreed to preach eight sermons on the nature, methods, and motives of early piety, I did, with satisfaction, look on their agreement as a motion from God. I could have no greater joy than to see my children thus walking in the truth, so zealous to invite and persuade others to choose the way of truth and walk with the God of their fathers. They have solicited a line or two from my aged and now shaking hand to indicate my satisfaction in what they have done, and I cheerfully give it.

Piety, or the return of a soul to God in His Christ, and a godly, sober, and righteous life led upon it, is the whole duty and interest, and wisdom of man. The earlier the piety, the greater the wisdom and comfort and glory of them that come into it. These are things that cannot be spoken against!

I therefore recommend this book of early piety, not only unto the young people in the country, but also unto their parents. I advise them to recommend it unto their families, and make it accompany the charges which they lay upon their children, to know and serve the God of their fathers.

As for me, I am now in the eighty-third year of my age. I have had an opportunity to converse with the most renowned servants of God, who were the first planters of this country and of the churches in it. I have been, for sixty-five years, a preacher of the gospel in these churches, except for certain years when I was favored by God with opportunities to serve Him in Europe. As a young man, I ministered in Dublin, in Gloucester, and in Guernsey, before the year 1662.

Thirty years later, after four years in an agency for the country, I cannot help but be in the disposition of those ancient men who had seen the foundation of the first temple, and wept with a loud voice to see how changed the rebuilt temple was. I wish it were nothing but the weakness of Horace's old man, the *Laudator Temporis acti*[1], when I complain that there is a grievous decay of piety in

---

1. Lit. *"one who praises past times."*

the land, and a leaving of the first love, and that the beauties of holiness are not to be seen in our churches, as once they were. A fruitful Christian has become too rare a spectacle. Yea, too many are given to change and leave that order of the gospel to set up and uphold which was the very design of these Colonies, and the very interest of New England seems to be changed from a religious to a worldly interest. It is to be feared that awful changes are further coming on the country, and that the Holy Son of God, offended at the apostasy, may order for it a deep share of the cup of trembling, which He is now giving to the sinful nations. I must weep, and I now do it with a loud voice, for what I see. *"Oh! That my head were waters, and my eyes a fountain of tears"* (Jer, 9:1)! Nothing will contribute so much to avert evil as a revival of piety, even of early piety, in the rising generation.

My own poor essays to that purpose have been published and repeated, and some of them reprinted many years ago. Now, I earnestly pray to the God of all grace, that He would succeed these holy labors of my sons, to serve the same designs of early piety.

I will call them my sons because, the first of them (being fifty-eight years old) is by nature so and has for forty-one years served with me in the gospel. The rest of them are such that I love them as my children. They are all faithful servants of God, and precious gifts of our ascended Savior unto His churches. They have all heretofore, given to the public in the way of the press desireable fruits and proofs of their abilities, some of which have been upon the subject of early piety. And what acceptable words must these preachers bring when they have been such laudable examples themselves in their own practice of that early piety which they thus preach unto others!

I am going the way of all the earth, and have been many years longing for that blessed hour when I shall (I have a good hope through grace) be received into the Everlasting Habitations and into that World which has no sin, and no temptation to sin in it, and where Christ is to be seen in His wondrous glories. But thou, O Lord, how long!

As Polycarp going to die gave his testimony that he had served Christ more than eighty years and had always found in Him a good master, so I would now also die bearing my testimony for Him, who in my early youth mercifully seized me for Himself, that in all my pilgrimage I have also found that glorious Lord to be a good Master. But though I do not know now how good a Master I shall find Him, I shall know hereafter. I shall not know, till He sends for me! Which, O my God and Savior, I am daily waiting for. Why is Thy chariot so long in coming? Why tarry the wheels of Thy chariot?

Increase Mather
Boston, July 4, 1721

TABLE of CONTENTS

Introduction
For People Raised in Christian Homes 13

Preface
By Dr. Increase Mather 15

Sermon 1
The Pious Parent's Wishes, by Dr. Cotton Mather 21

Sermon 2
The Nature of Early Piety as It Respects God, by Mr. Wadsworth 41

Sermon 3
Early Piety as It Respects Men, by Mr. Colman 59

Sermon 4
Early Piety as it Respects Ourselves, by Mr. Sewall 79

Sermon 5
The Obligations to Early Piety, by Mr. Prince 97

Sermon 6
The Advantages of Early Piety, by Mr. Webb 127

Sermon 7
Objections Answered, by Mr. Cooper 149

Sermon 8
Exhortations and Directions to Young People, by Mr. Foxcroft 169

Preface to the Final Chapter
That You Might Receive Dr. Increase Mather's Testimony 205

Sermon 9
Advice to the Children of Godly Ancestors, by Dr. Increase Mather 207

KNOWING *the* STATE *of* YOUR SOUL

Dr. Cotton Mather, Boston, January 23, 1721

1 Chronicles 29:19
Give my son Solomon a loyal heart

The Blessing of Early Piety: What Will Make You Happy

O blessed and hopeful children, and what comforts to their parents, that are made partakers of such a blessing! O blessed and joyful parents, that may see such a blessing obtained for their children! Early piety is the glorious blessedness. There is an unspeakable passion in the souls of parents to see their children happy. Nature knows not a passion more vehement, more engaging. I am going to show you, O children, what will make you happy. I am going to show you, O parents, how you may come to see them happy. O set your hearts unto these things, for your life is in them. Give a great attention. But, O gracious God, make Thou a good impression upon the hearers of them!

A Coin

I remember that on a coin of the emperor Constans, there is the emperor drawing a youth after him, and those words about him, *Faelix Temporum Reparatio*[1], intimating that for the reforming of the times, youth is principally to be dealt withal. Sensible of this, the managers of your lectures propose now a set of sermons on early piety, hoping in and waiting on heaven, to give an efficacy to them.

We find that the illustrious David, a little before he died, was very solicitous about the welfare of the son that was to survive him and succeed him. David desired to have the son, whom his own eyes and the eyes of the people were much upon, do worthily after he should die.

---

1. Lit. *"happy renewal of times"*

A Call To God

Behold, first, the method that is taken by a father full of goodness, so that he might have a happy son, and that a son should be like him. He prays for the son. He carries him to God. He commits him to God. He intreats God mercifully to take notice of him. No other method is like this.

The Blessing to Seek

But then, behold, the second blessing to be sought in this method is the blessing that alone makes a happy son. A perfect heart is that blessing. Here, a perfect heart is desired for Solomon, a thing enough to make a happy Solomon! The name of Solomon is derived from the word that signifies to be perfect, as well as to be peaceable. It is, as if David says, *"Lord, make my Solomon a real Solomon, give to my Solomon the heart of a Solomon, let the heart as well as the name of my son, have that perfection."*

I again tell you that a pious mind is the thing to be understood by a perfect heart, and this is the doctrine which now very strongly demands a devout reception with you.

A Perfect Heart

The pious mind, of a perfect heart, will make blessed children, and parents ought fervently to pour out their prayer unto the God of all grace, to pour down such a blessing upon their children.

It will be proper, in the first place, to declare what that blessing is, which, being found in our children, they will be known to be an offspring that the Lord has blessed. Children, a perfect heart must be found in you, if you would not incur the doom of cursed children. I tell you again and again that a pious mind is that perfect heart.

A principle of piety, infused into the heart, is that which will make it a perfect heart. We do not expect from you an absolute perfection, which the heart of no man in this world may pretend unto; or a heart perfectly, completely, exactly, and in all points conformed unto the law of God that no man in this world has attained. Since the fall of man, there never was but one Man whose heart complied with the will of God in all things, and He was more than a mere man. It was He who, with a perfect heart, wrought out and brought in the righteousness which alone you are to plead before God, O our children, that you may be justified. Who can say, *"I have made my heart clean?"* However, there is an evangelical perfection that will be expected and required of you.

Otherwise, Hezekiah, who was no old man, could not have made such an appeal to the glorious God, as in Isaiah 38:3: *"O Lord, I pray, how I have walked before You in truth and with a loyal heart, and have done what is good in Your sight."* Truly, such a heart is produced, where a principle of piety is in its operation.

Thorough Conversion

Wherefore, first, O children, if you would have a perfect heart, you must make sure of a hearty, real, and thorough conversion unto God. You read of such an excellent thing as in Ezekiel 36:26: *"I will give you a new heart and put a new spirit within you."* This new heart will be a perfect one: a changed heart, a cleansed heart, a heart with a new inclination upon it, a heart no longer set upon the vanities of the world; a heart wherein God resumes His throne and idols are dethroned, and God has the regards paid unto Him which have heretofore been sinfully paid unto creatures. This is the perfect heart.

A heart filled with the love of God and set above all things, to choose and to do the things that please Him; a heart filled with the love of Christ, and closing with Him in all His offices, and feeding and living on the fullness of which there is all in Him; a heart filled with the love which is due to mankind, and which will make one do as He would be done unto. This is the pious mind, which, O children, you must come into if you would not perish wonderfully.

Signs of Conversion

There will be a perfect heart in this pious mind. There will be a true conversion to piety, which will reach to every faculty of the heart. The new creature, in the converts of Zion, is perfect in that it has every part, though the renovation be but in part. A young person brought home to God has his understanding enlightened, his fantasy regulated, his memory purified, his will rectified, his affections brought into order. He gives up his whole heart unto God. He reserves no powers of his mind, but concerning all of them, He says, *"Oh! Let my Saviour take possession of it."*

Sincerity

Secondly, as we would bring our children to a profession of piety, so we would exhort them to sincerity in their profession. Children, get a sincere heart and you will have a perfect heart. Sincerity has a sort of perfection in it. You must have your heart engaged in what you do about the service of God. When He calls, as in Proverbs 23:26, *"My son, give me your heart,"* your heart must reply, *"My God, I am entirely thine!"* The heart as well as the name is to be given unto the Lord.

Banishing Offensiveness

The heart is to be washed from wickedness, and everything that is offensive unto God must be banished from it. This is a perfect heart. A young person of such a pious mind will realize the eye of God upon him and will behave himself as having his very heart naked and open before Him. *"Walk before me and be blameless"* (Gen. 17:1), said our God unto the patriarch Abraham. Children, you must walk as before God, doing that which is right and having a right aim in your doing of it. Sincerely aim at offering up to God an acceptable sacrifice, not aiming at the praise of men in what you do and not merely seeking to avoid the censures of your superiors or your observers in what you do.

Obedience

Thirdly, we cannot be satisfied, except our children endeavor to have a universal obedience unto God. What is a perfect heart? Children, you will be before God what you desire, and study, and labor to be. You ought to mightily and constantly strive after a perfect heart and a perfection of obedience to God. You have those two together in 1 Chronicles 28:9: My son, *"know the God of your father, and serve Him with a loyal heart and with a willing mind."* Your heart will be perfect if your mind is willing to be and to do all that you find God enjoining upon you.

A young person willing to be made perfect and whole, lacking nothing in his obedience to God, willing and wishing to be made perfect in every good work, doing the will of God, denying all ungodliness and leading a godly, sober, and righteous life, this is one of a perfect heart. This, who if he might have his will, would never sin against the God that is above, one who makes it his exercise to keep a conscience void of offence towards God and man. O! May you all, with such a pious mind, have respect unto all the commandments of God!

A Heart Fixed on Holiness

Finally, O our children, being thus disposed for piety, and resolved for the ways of God, we must have you fixed in your holy resolutions, with a humble dependence on your Savior for the aids of His grace. You must come to that place as expressed in Psalm 57:7: *"My heart is steadfast, O God, my heart is steadfast."* It is a heart fixed for God. This fixed heart will be a perfect heart. You must not only begin well, but hold on and hold out unto the end. A pious mind will be sure to do so, and will, with a patient continuance in well-doing, lay hold on eternal life. The apostasy of Solomon was very disagreeable to the perfect heart that the prayer of his father begged on his behalf. But then in his recovery out of his apostasy, we may hope that the prayer was answered.

This is the blessing that will invest our children with all blessings, all the blessings of goodness are comprehended in it. Now, you parents, what shall you do that your children may be enriched with it?

Fervent Prayer

You are required to pour out your fervent prayer to the God of all grace that He would pour down the blessing of a perfect heart and a pious mind upon your children. Godly parents will cry to God, *"Oh! That my offspring may live in Thy sight!"* They will keep crying to Him till their weeping faith has received this answer from Him: *"As for your offspring, I have heard thee! Behold, I have blessed them."*

Personal Holiness

Parents, what is your main concern for your children? Piety in you will make it your main concern that your children may have a pious mind. If your main concern is to get the rubies of this world for your children and leave a belly full of this world unto them, it looks very suspiciously as if you were yourselves the people of this world, whose portion is only in this life. Most certainly, you are earthly-minded ones, if your main concern for your children is that they may have the fine things of the earth heaped upon them. Your own heart is not right in the sight of God if you are not thoroughly persuaded to desire that your children be enriched with a perfect heart rather for them to be supplied with silver and with gold, or with any perishable riches. You are directed to Matthew 6:33: *"Seek first the kingdom of God and His righteousness."* The directive is that you do so for the sake of your children, as well as for yourselves. Oh! Seek first that which a righteous individual with a pious mind would seek after, that your children may be brought into the Kingdom of God. We read indeed, that wisdom is good with an inheritance, but what good will any temporal inheritance do them if your children are not made wise unto salvation?

Parents, if you have a perfect heart yourselves, nothing but such a heart in your children can make you be at peace about them. If you can easily bear to see your children without it, you are yourselves without the fear of God.

Mourn Over Them

We read in Proverbs 17:25 that a *"foolish son is a grief to his father, and bitterness to her who bore him."* To have a son take such a course, he must be mourned over as another Absalom. To have a daughter so lewd, and so base, you must complain, *"Alas, my daughter, thou hast brought me low, and thou art one of them who trouble me."*

What a grievous bitterness must such a thing be to godly parents. This is the thing to be again and again urged upon you. Lift up a prayer, yea a cry that shall reach and pierce the heavens unto the glorious Lord: *"Lord, give Thou a perfect heart unto mine offspring."*

Call for Compassion

The parents of old came unto our Savior with their children that had maladies or were seized by evil spirits, and He had compassion on them. Oh, implore this compassion on them. Oh, implore this compassion of your Savior for your children. A pious mind would relieve all their maladies, would rescue them from all evil spirits, and would make lovely and happy children of them. The matter is to be yet more distinctly communicated with several admonitions.

Acknowledge Sin Passed On

First, I pray, what is that heart which these poor children of yours are born with? Truly, such a one as you know, that you before them were born with a sinful heart, a corrupt heart, a vicious heart, and a heart that is a very hell of wickedness. What are your children by nature? This nature, as the poison of the old serpent entered into our first parents, has also entered them. It is a sad relation which the oracles of God have given of it in Ephesians 2:3. They are *"by nature children of wrath."*

What is the heart that your children bring into the world with them? A heart that is deceitful above all things, and desperately wicked. An evil heart of unbelief that always departs from the living God. It is the same heart that the people before the flood were infected with: *"Every intent of the thoughts of his heart was only evil continually"* (Gen. 6:5). O wretched heart! Who and what shall deliver your children from such a heart? How can you bear to see them lie in these deadly circumstances, thus dead in trespasses and sins? A perfect heart will be the only deliverance of your children from this wretched heart. Nothing but a pious mind and a sanctifying work of God upon the heart can bring the heart of your children out of the woeful depravation that sin has brought upon them.

O parents, you ought to be concerned all the more to seek this deliverance for them, inasmuch as it is through your mediation that this distempered heart is conveyed unto them. 'Tis a hereditary distemper; through your loins it is conveyed. The best of parents have such a heart-breaking thought as this to humble them. Even the son of Jesse the righteous, did say, *"I was brought forth in iniquity, and in sin my mother conceived me"* (Ps. 51:5). Oh! You ought to do all that can be done, that the heart of your children may be cured of the leprosy, and the grievous diseases, which you have given them!

It was a fair law concerning the man that had wounded another given in Exodus 21:19: He *"shall provide for him to be thoroughly healed."* What! Will you not do what you can, that your children may be thoroughly healed of the wounds given them of which you yourselves are an accessory? O worthy are you to be called killers rather than parents! How can you see the forlorn state of your children and not have your heart bleeding over them.

Providing for Your Child

Secondly, once you may see a perfect heart in your children, you will see them therein provided for? Parents, if you will not provide for your children, what are you? Ostriches, nay, infidels! Nor is this term hard enough. You have the brand of such in 1 Timothy 5:8: *"If anyone does not provide for his own, and especially for those of his household, he has denied the faith and is worse than an unbeliever."* If your children once came to have a perfect heart in them, they are well provided for, but never until then! The Hebrew word for *"peace,"* comes from this root, *"shalam,"* to be perfect.

Verily, they that have a perfect heart have a root of peace within them - a root that all the peaceable fruits of righteousness will grow upon. A perfect peace will be that which a perfect heart will have a claim to. A perfect heart is that godliness which has the promise, both of the life that now is, and of that which is to come. It is promised unto the upright.

A Godly Heritage

The Lord God is a sun and a shield. The Lord will give grace and glory. It may be that you cannot lay up any great portion of wealth for your children. But oh, if they have a perfect heart, your children will have a portion and a godly heritage. Yea, the infinite God Himself is their portion. Then you may be sure that God will be their Father, and their Father will know what they want and grant it unto them. You may be sure, that when father and mother forsake them, the Lord will take them up. Yea, then you may be sure, that they are not brought forth for the murderer. You may be sure, that they shall be blessed with all the spiritual blessings in the heavenly places. You may be sure they shall have a share in the inheritance of the saints in light, and one day come to inherit all things. Oh! The glad parents that can see their children thus admirably provided for!

Children Destitute of a Perfect Heart

Thirdly, if your children remain destitute of a perfect heart, their condition is deplorable, miserable beyond all expression! Parents, can you see your children in slavery to the powers of darkness, serving diverse lusts, and not be in anguish to see them set at liberty? Can you see your children, fallen into the cruel fangs of lions or of tigers, and not with agony call for some help unto them? Can you see your children fast asleep in a house on fire over their heads, and not fly with agony to help them out of the flames? This is their very condition. And nothing, I say unto you, nothing but a perfect heart brought into them can save them out of it.

Dying in Their Sins

Strangers to a perfect heart, they die in their sins. They die, so that it would have been better for them if they had never been born. This will be the state of you and your children if they never have a perfect heart produced in them. Your children have upon them the spots that show they are not the children of God, until a perfect heart has taken away those ugly and filthy spots.

The hearts of your children have in them the seeds of eternal death, the worms that will never die. The dispositions in the carnal mind of your children are such that they cannot please God in them. They are full of enmity to God.

A Perfect Heart

The holy God can be no other but a consuming fire unto them, until they have a heart otherwise disposed. God will be terrible to them in His holy places, The holy places themselves cannot but be terrible, uneasy, ungrateful to them. They will not be able to breathe in so pure an element. Nothing but a perfect heart can save them from the wrath to come. They are fuel for the devouring fire and the everlasting burnings, until a perfect heart has given another temper to them. Oh! If you would not have your children cast into the place of dragons, you must be in pain to get a perfect heart into them. They are undone, undone until this is done for them.

Fourthly, where is the perfect heart? Where does it come from? Who gives it? Surely, none but the God of all grace can give it. It is the glorious God who says, *"I will give you a new heart and put a new spirit within you"* (Ezek. 36:26). If we could give a perfect heart unto our children ourselves and fill their heart with the love of their God and their neighbor and a zeal to do good, what virtuous parents would not presently do it with all their heart?

"Lord, it should be the first thing that we would presently do for our children, to make them Thy children." But it is beyond us, it is above us. A very distinguishing stroke and beat of a perfect heart is a faith in the only Savior, a flight unto Him for His great salvation. But whose gift is this! We are told in Ephesians 2:8: *"It is the gift of God."* We are elsewhere told more than once that God gives repentance. A perfect heart, which is always a very tender one, it is a stone turned into flesh. Who but the almighty God can do such a thing as that? Create in us a clean heart, O our God. It is a creating work, to make a perfect heart. None but God the Creator of all things can do such a thing. *"This is My glory,"* says the Lord, *"And My glory I will not give unto another."*

The Necessity of Prayer

Fifthly, is not this the way to obtain this gift, prayer to the God of all grace; by pouring out your prayer to a gracious God for it. We are taught concerning the blessing of a perfect heart in Ezekiel 36:37: *"I will also let the house of Israel inquire of Me to do this for them."* When parents, with unceasing fervor, implore our good God, that He would please to do this good unto their children, to make them good and upright in heart, He will, at some time or another, do it for them.

The Willingness of God

Our good God is willing to bestow the grace of a perfect heart when He is asked for it. Nay, there is no case, wherein that word is oftener fulfilled, than it is in this: *"Ask, and it will be given to you"* (Matt. 7:7). Nor is there any prayer more grateful unto God than this.

Parents, there is nothing for which you can go to God with more encouragement and expectation, *"O do Thou give a perfect heart unto this child, the heart of Thy children, O my God."* I can lead you to a word worth more than a rock of diamonds or a mountain of gold! It is that word given in Luke 11:13: *"If you then, being evil, know how to give good gifts to your children, how much more will your heavenly Father give the Holy Spirit to those who ask Him!"*

What a ravishing word this is! Quickened by it, oh, go now to your heavenly

Father, not only for yourselves, but also for your children. With tears beg it of Him: *"O my Father, I long, I long for it, that my children may be Thy servants. O my Savior, if Thou will allow of it, the descent of Thy Holy Spirit upon them, will make them so. O my God, let thy good Spirit lead them into the land of rectitude. O Spirit of grace, do thou take possession of them."* 'Tis very certain, that if God gives His Holy Spirit unto your children, the Holy Spirit will give a perfect heart unto them.

The Spirit's Work

The Holy Spirit will renew a right spirit in them, will purify their heart by a faith of His working there, and will make them the temples of God. The Holy Spirit will write His laws in their heart, and rectify all disorders there, and bring all things to rights within them. Yea, as we read, that when the Holy Spirit first fell on the Gentiles, the spectators were astonished at what they saw. When the Holy Spirit falls on your children, you will see things done for them that will fill you with astonishment. What satisfaction! Oh, What consolation! Ask, ask, and see what will be done for you. But, it must be remembered, that your prayer for the renovation of your children and their passing from death to life, must have two components.

Persistent Prayer

First, your Savior has told you that men ought always to pray and not to faint. Your prayers for your children must be persistent, that type which a compassionate heaven usually gives no denial to! Prayers and supplications, with strong crying and tears, to Him that is able to save your children from the death which you are afraid will feed upon them! Oh! Plead with a compassionate God as a soul wrestling with Him and weeping in supplications, that will humbly protest, *"Lord, I will not let Thee go except Thou bless the children, and put Thy fear into them!"*

Humbly plead with Him for His promise, and show Him His own handwriting, even that word on which He has caused you to hope from Isaiah 44:3: *"I will pour My Spirit on your descendants, and My blessing on your offspring."* Do thus, until the newborn child shall be called a Samuel, and you may say, *"I have asked him and gained him of the Lord."* But then, the persistence of your prayers must especially be expressed in the perpetuity of them. The mercy of seeing your children turned from darkness unto light, and from the power of Satan unto God, perhaps will not be presently granted you.

A God who waits that He may be gracious, will have this mercy waited for. If you don't grow weary of calling upon God, but still follow Him with your incessant prayers, O you that keep sowing in tears, you shall see a comfortable harvest; you shall find that the Lord is good unto them that wait for him, unto the soul that seeks him.

Hold On and Pray

There will be a month, wherein God will find these wild children and make new creatures of them. It may be, O Hezekiah, that God will bind thy wicked Manasseh into the chains of such afflictions or such convictions, as will compel him to seek the God of his father (II Chron. 32:33-33:9). My friend, crying to thy Savior that thy child may be freed from the devils that have possession of it, He may appear deaf unto your cry. But still, hold on! Hold on! Pray on! O my Savior have mercy on my sinful child, and let no devil detain him from Thy service! Do so until thou hear Him say, *"Great is thy faith; be it unto thee as thou wilt!"*

Take Action

Secondly, your efforts must accompany your prayers. You must instruct your children, you must advise your children as well as pray for them, speak to them as well as for them. You must restrain them, and use all the methods of prudence to keep them from the paths of the destroyer. Use all the methods of wisdom to win their souls and spread the nets of salvation for them.

Command Them

Do not only pray for your children, but also lay the charges of God upon them like David who charged Solomon, his son, and said, *"Keep the charge of the Lord your God: to walk in His ways"* (1 Kings 2:3).

Oh! With all possible solemnity, lay upon them those charges from 1 Chronicles 28:9: *"Know the God of your father, and serve Him with a loyal heart and with a willing mind."* Take them aside and charge them to immediately consider their ways and look into the state of their souls. Charge those with distressed souls to embrace an offered Savior with all His benefits. Charge them to keep up the religion of the closet and read the Word, and seek the face of God in their daily retirements. And charge them to shun dangerous company, to forsake the foolish and live and remember the bonds of God that were laid upon them in their baptism. Yea, then cause them to kneel down by you, and make them the witnesses of the weeping supplications with which you carry them unto the Lord. Not only the servants, but also the handmaids of the Lord have done thus, and the success of it on their children has been admirable!

Set the Pattern

But then there is one thing more to be expected from you. Parents, be patterns; let your children see in you the patterns of all goodness. Be exemplary, with holiness in all manner of conversation, give them an example of a prayerful, watchful, fruitful walk with God. In you, let them see how they should walk, that God may be pleased with them. When Elisha was concerned for a double portion of the Spirit that had been in his predecessor, Elijah told him that, if He saw him at his mounting up to heaven, He should have it. This may be, and has been so far alluded to. If your children may see you going to heaven, see the heavenly flights of your souls, your contempt of earth, your horror at sin, your value for Christ, and your communion with God, there would probably fall upon them a mighty portion of the spirit which you desire for them, the spirit of piety.

The Response

It is now time for our children to become sensible of an inference, which there can be no avoiding. Certainly, O children, you should be as much concerned for yourselves as you see your parents are for you. You ought fervently to make your own prayer, to the God of all grace, for that perfect heart and pious mind which your parents are seeking for you. 'Tis what I am now to press upon the young people in the auditory: Oh! Let it become your heart's desire, and your prayer unto God that a perfect heart may be given unto you. Fall down before the glorious God, to bestow all the dispositions of a pious mind upon thee! If any of you lack this wisdom, let them ask it of God, and it shall be given them. Think not to say within yourselves that because you have parents who have prayed for you, there is no need of your praying for yourselves. For I say unto you, that if you have not so much tendency to a pious mind as to pray for a pious mind yourselves, and if the fruits of a pious mind be not found upon you, God will bow you down and cast you into a fire that never shall be quenched.

The Rising Generation

There is a passage in the Psalms which a famous Jew would have read thus: *"It is time for You to act, O Lord, for they have regarded Your law as void"* (Ps. 119:126).

The men without whose vision the people would perish do see a sad spectacle in the rising generation among us. They see vast numbers of young people with madness in their heart, going down unto the dead. They see busy apostles of Satan using various arts to render the ministry of the gospel despicable, and even detestable unto them, and so utterly defeat the hopes of their being brought home unto God. They see little foxes using more than little attempts to spoil the vines, sour, and wither the tender grapes, to turn them into the grapes of Sodom. The eye affects the heart of these righteous men, and they weep in secret places, to see the souls of the children ripening for a wrath unto the uttermost and spiritual plagues worse than brimstone scattered on our habitations.

Wherefore, it is time to work for the Lord, and a very considerable stroke of the work, which our hand finds to do, is to prevail with you, O our exposed children. We seek that you get a pious mind and that you do with your might what you have to do, for the obtaining and expressing of such a mind before your going down to the grave.

Children, oh the perfect heart which has been commended unto you, don't you hear the heart-melting sighs of heaven over you? *"Oh! That there were such a heart in them; that they would fear me… that it might go well with the children forever"*(Deut. 5:29)!

A Pious Mind

The pious mind would raise you to that inestimable dignity. *"You are my sons and my daughters,"* says the Lord Almighty! The pious mind that would fetch down from the throne of God these joyful tidings to you, child, be of good cheer, thy sins are forgiven thee! The pious mind, that would so adorn you, as to procure that applause for you, soul, thou art a daughter of God, all glorious within, and the king shall greatly desire thy beauty. The pious mind that would recommend you to the angels as the guardians which would make all things work together to our good, and invite those morning stars to sing together over you, arise, and shine, for thy light is come, and the glory of the Lord is risen upon thee!

When shall this wisdom enter into your hearts? When will you get this wisdom? It is the principal thing. It would be a good step if you would esteem it so. Yea, we should, with a glad heart, if we saw the beginning of a pious mind in you, if we saw you beginning to go and pray and weep unto your Savior for it. This grace begins in the desires of the grace! It was once appealed in Nehemiah 1:11: *"O Lord, I pray, please let Your ear be attentive to the prayer of Your servant, and to the prayer of Your servants who desire to fear Your name."*

You begin to fear God, and are lifted among His true servants, when you desire to fear Him. Were this prayer made in earnest with you: *"Glorious God, change my heart, and bestow a pious mind upon me!"* Verily, that pious mind would be seen dawning in you that will shine more and more unto the perfect day. When God has wrought such desires in the mind of a young person, 'tis a token for good. He intends a blessed answer to them.

Children, Pray

Children, entreat us not to leave you or to return from following after you until we see our God becoming your God, and until we hear you with a pious mind calling upon Him for the grace of such a mind. On that passage of the preacher, the words of the wise are as goads, the ancients urge that our sermons ought to have pungencies in them. Children, there are pungent things to be now spoken to you. Oh! May two or three dissuasions make a strong impression upon you! We read indeed of a fiery brute, that He believes not the sound of the trumpet, the thunder of the captains, and the shouting. But oh! Foolhardy youths, be not as the horse that has no understanding, for there shall be many sorrows to such wicked fools. You that now mock at thunderbolts may think to mock on, but your mocking is very near to a catastrophe. God will change it into mourning for you. God will with swift executions bring upon you things that should be trembled at.

Three Questions

In the meantime, there are some awful questions to be trembled at. I will demand of thee, O young one, walking in the way of thine own heart. I will demand of thee, and answer thou me. But if you decline to answer my questions, the great God shall from the sacred place of thunder answer them.

Question I: How Much Time Do You Have?

Are you sure, that you shall have any more time, than this very moment allowed you, to make sure of what you may in a pious mind be brought unto? Is there any report more common than this: *"Their young ones are dead."* Is not our Golgotha full of graves, that reach not unto your conversation? Of the six thousand, four hundred or so that have died in our city within twenty years, (besides our very many young men who have died abroad) there were probably not more than three thousand, who had not reached unto their middle age! If you harden your hearts and refuse today to hear His voice, how do you know, but the angel of death may stand by your bedsides, and with an uplifted hand swear by Him who lives forever and ever, that you shall no longer have time to live and have order to strike you down immediately? Is any of you all assured of this, that this is not the last sermon that shall ever call upon you?

Unto this question, hear the answer of God: *"Do not boast about tomorrow, for you do not know what a day may bring forth"* (Prov. 27:1).

Question II: What Will Be Your End?

If you die in your sins, without that holiness of a pious mind without which no man shall see the Lord, what will become of you? Can any imagination yet clothed in flesh, form a clear and full notion of what you must endure in the strange punishment, reserved for the workers of iniquity? But are there not great plagues and of a long continuance, which you must look for, tremendous things to be done unto you by the hands of an infinite God, resolving to have a triumph of His justice, in what He will do upon you if you go away unreconciled unto Him? Unto this question, hear the answer of God: *"It is a fearful thing to fall into the hands of the living God"* (Heb. 10:31).

Question III: How Great Will Be Your Torment?

If you are the children of parents who have been themselves of a pious mind, and who have done a great deal to bring you unto a pious mind, but you remain impenitent after all, must not you receive a greater damnation than any other children in the world? If you go on to grieve your parents, what a vengeance will pursue such children! If you go on still in your trespasses, what wounds will your aggravated impieties expose you to? In the torments of hell, are there any who do under more flaming tortures cry out, *"I am tormented in this flame,"* than such as have a father Abraham, and religious ancestors to make a bitter mention of? How will you bear the many stripes, which by sinning against what you know to be the will of God, you will bring upon your unhappy souls? How will you bear to hear the sentence of the eternal judgment, and those that were your loving, tender, heart-broken parents acquiescing in it!

The great God answers the question in Proverbs 1:25-26: *"Because you disdained all my counsel, and would have none of my rebuke, I also will laugh at your calamity; I will mock when your terror comes."*

Consider these things, O young people, consider, lest the Glorious One, exasperated by your impenitence, tear you to pieces and there be none to deliver you!

Be Thoughtful

We read in Proverbs 1:4, to *"The young man knowledge and discretion."* The Hebrew word which we render *"discretion"* may be rendered *"thoughtfulness."* How discreet and how pious would our young people soon become, if they would but grow thoughtful and ponder the paths of their feet, and think on what is before them!

Regarding what a young man coming to be what he should be, and what, O young people, we wish you all to be, we read Luke 15:17: *"He came to himself."* Oh! That the experiment might now be made among our children who are exceeding mad and will continue to be so until a perfect heart brings the young ones to be sober minded. This is what we now exhort them to. It may be, my child, a little consideration that may bring you to yourself and upon it, we should soon see you in a right mind and with a perfect heart coming to bless the Most High and praise Him that liveth forever and ever.

Consider Heaven

Wherefore, first, in an earnest consideration, take the wings of the morning and fly up to the heavenly world. Consider the glorious things that are spoken about the city of God, and how your early piety will allow you to enjoy the mansions there. Walk about that Zion, the city of the living God; go round about her, consider her palaces and see what is done by the great God there for them who early take Him as their own God and their guide unto death and beyond. Think, *"If I go up to that world, I shall see a perfect rest from every thing that can here be uneasy to me. I shall have no sorrow there, but all tears shall be wiped from my eyes."*

Think again, *"If I go up to that world, I shall find in the all-sufficient God, all that is relishable and valuable in any creatures here, and inconceivably more. An admirable Christ will fill me with all the fullness of God."* Think once more, *"If I go up to that world, I shall reap a full harvest of all my patient continuance in well-doing and let me now abound in the work of the Lord. I shall then find my labor not in vain for the Lord."* And then let your consideration lead you to the eternity that that world will be brightened and sweetened with, the duration of your felicity in the everlasting habitations, and the eternal glory to which the God of all grace will call you when He brings you into early piety. Think, *"If I come to be comforted in that world, it will be with an everlasting consolation. The fountains of living water to which I shall be led will be running forevermore. My knowledge will be eternally progressive, my delight will be eternally varied. After I have been satisfying myself in the eternal God, for as many millions of ages as there are now beams of light in the world, I shall be no nearer to the end of my satisfaction, than I was to the first moment of my entering into the joy of my Lord."*

Consider Hell

But then, go on; let your consideration remove the bars of the pits, and uncover the dismal vault, and look down into the infernal world. Consider the tremendous things which are inflicted on the despisers of early piety, who for being so, shall be condemned and confined unto that place of torment. Visit the gloomy and howling regions, where God sets those in dark places, who have been dead of old. God hedges them about. They cannot get out. God makes their chain heavy. When they cry and shout, He shuts out their prayer. God is as a lion unto them in the secret places; He pulls them in pieces and makes them desolate. God causes the arrows of His quiver to enter into them, and He fills them with bitterness. Think, *"If I must go down to that world, I shall carry with me the raging desires of the diverse lusts which I am now serving. But they will only help to torture me, and I shall not have so much as a drop of water to gratify them. I shall be unstable and hungry, and fret myself, and curse God, and look upward. And when I look back unto the earth, and remember the good things I received there, oh! The dimness of the anguish I shall have upon me, finding my self driven into darkness."*

Think again, *"If I go down to that world, all the pains that ever I did or could suffer by the mediation of my senses here, I shall have more immediately dispensed unto me there, in very tormenting sentiments which a provoked God will compel me to, and all those pains are little enough to punish my crimes in denying the God that is above."* Think once more, *"If I go down to that world, an Almighty God Himself will take me into His own hands, and make me feel such scalding strokes of His wrath as no tongue is able to express, no heart is able to conceive. Immediate emanations from an offended, omnipotent, omnipresent God will penetrate like lightening into my soul. Immediate flashes from God act as a consuming fire. God himself will fight against me with a strong arm, and in great wrath. Can my hands be strong and my heart endure, when God shall deal with me?"*

But then, let your consideration remind you of the eternity that renders that world yet more terrible, the everlasting punishment which the wicked haters of God and of early piety shall go down into. Think, *"If I come to be tormented in the flames of that world, I know not of any end of my torment. An aching tooth for one month, how tedious would it be unto me here! But if I lie down among the damned, I must undergo much worse griefs than that, and after as many millions of years as there are leaves on the trees or drops in the sea or sands in the shore, I have no prospect of any relief. The Mediator delivering up His kingdom, I shall be left still under the vengeance of God, with no intercessor for me, laid in the lowest pit, shut up, where I cannot come forth any more."*

Let the young person thus muse till the fire burns. It may be hoped, the issue will be, he considers and he turns! The issue would be, that, from this time, the young person with a perfect heart will say unto God, *"Lord, Thou art my Father. Thou art my Savior, Thou shall be the guide of my youth."*

Take Action

Children, let not your concern for a perfect heart be put off upon the pretence, *"I can do nothing of myself, nor can I change my own heart."* Our Savior bids the man that had a withered hand, *"Stretch out your hand."* Instead of making an excuse, *"Lord, I cannot,"* he tried it, and he did it. Make the effort, O soul, upon a return to God. Test whether you can pray for a perfect heart with cries that shall pierce the heavens. And then test whether that withered hand of yours becomes so enlivened by Him as to take hold on His covenant, and thereby lay hold on eternal life and come to those motions of early piety which nothing but a perfect heart ever comes unto. Try, oh! Try whether with a perfect heart you can come to this, and set thy heart (yea, your very hand) unto such an instrument as this: *"Great God, I am willing that Thou should be my God. Great God, Thou hast made me willing to be Thy servant. Blessed Savior, Thou hast conquered my soul, and I am willing, that Thou should make me righteous and make me holy. Reconcile the great God unto me, and enable me to live unto Him."*

the **BLESSING** *of the* **FEAR** *of the* **LORD**

Benjamin Wadsworth, Boston, March 30, 1720

Psalm 34:11
Come, you children, listen to me; I will teach you the fear of the Lord.

The title of this Psalm shows that holy David was the author of it. When he had been in eminent danger among the Philistines, God graciously and wonderfully delivered him, and his heart was filled with holy gratitude to God for this deliverance. He said in verse one, *"I will bless the LORD at all times; His praise shall continually be in my mouth"* (Ps. 34:1). He stirred up himself and others to bless and praise God for the great deliverance God had favored him with. Verse three says, *"Oh, magnify the Lord with me, and let us exalt His name together"* (Ps. 34:3). Indeed, God, the inexhaustible fountain of living waters, is freely and communicatively good to all that sincerely seek and serve Him. David therefore exhorts to such a seeking and serving of God. Verses 8-10 state: *"Oh, taste and see that the LORD is good; blessed is the man who trusts in Him! Oh, fear the Lord, you His saints! There is no want to those who fear Him. The young lions lack and suffer hunger; but those who seek the Lord shall not lack any good thing"* (Ps. 34:8-10). Our text itself is of the same general strain, namely, to incite and quicken others to seek and serve God. David says, *"Come you children, listen to me; I will teach you the fear of the Lord"* (Ps. 34:11). David, by God's command, was appointed king (1 Sam. 16:12) and by His Spirit was made a prophet (Acts 2:29-30).

This holy man, this true saint, this royal prophet said: *"Come, you children"* (Ps. 34:11). He gives them the kind compellation of children that notes his tender paternal regard to them. *"As a father pities his children"* (Ps. 103:13), and the disposition which was (or should have been) in them, that is, that they were as pliable, tractable, and teachable as children are (or should be), ready to receive wholesome instructions, and with good impressions on their minds.

Come you children, come. Indeed, it is worth your while to come, well worth your while to hear, learn, and observe the things I have to teach you.

So children, mind what I say. It is well worth your while to come, to come from Sabbath to Sabbath, from lecture to lecture, to embrace all opportunities, to improve all proper seasons, to be instructed in, and quickened to, what is for the good of your souls, your precious immortal souls, which are of more worth than the world. *"Well,"* says David, *"come you children, and I will teach you."* Teach what? The fear of the Lord. He would teach them to be sincerely and practically religious, to know, trust in, love, fear, serve, and obey God, so as to be happy in His favor. He would teach them what was most needful, useful, and profitable to them.

Here we may observe that true saving graces are inseparably connected together, that they all spring from the same regenerating, renewing change wrought in the soul, from the image of God renewed in and impressed on the heart by the Holy Spirit. Where there is one saving grace, there are all saving graces. Agreeably we find, that the general comprehensive blessings of the new covenant are sometimes pronounced concerning persons as endowed with this or that particular grace. Thus, *"Blessed is the man who trusts in the LORD"* (Jer. 17:7). So, *"Eye has not seen, nor ear heard, nor have entered into the heart of man the things which God has prepared for those who love Him"* (1 Cor. 2:9).

Again, *"Blessed is the man who fears the LORD, who delights greatly in His commandments"* (Ps. 112:1). Therefore, by the fear of the Lord spoken of in our text, we may understand universal piety, including all that knowledge, faith, repentance, love, fear, hope, and holy obedience, holds for our happiness. The fear of the Lord, in our text, seems to be of the same type as Ecclesiastes 12:13: *"Fear God and keep His commandments, for this is man's all,"* or 1 Peter 1:17: *"Conduct yourselves throughout the time of your stay here in fear."* In fear, there is a conscientious regard to all that God teaches you and requires of you.

From the text thus opened, we might note that first, those who have true piety themselves (as the psalmist speaking in our text had), will be willing to be at pains to promote the same piety in others. If piety is suitably awake and active in them, they will not grudge taking pains to teach, exhort, and incite others to know and serve God. They will be for provoking others to love and good works (Heb. 10:24). They will have *"no greater joy than to hear that my children walk in truth"* (3 John 1:4).

Promote Early Piety

Secondly, so excellent is early piety that it is not beneath the greatest and best of men to endeavor to promote it. Though David was anointed to be king and was a prophet, he thought it not below or beneath him to instruct others, even young ones, children, to fear the Lord. I acknowledge, the word banime, *"sons,"* here rendered *"children."* Strictly taken, it is not limited to young ones, yet since it's here rendered *"children"* and may well extend to young ones, (though not exclusive of others), will at present speak to the text, chiefly as it concerns persons while young. Indeed, the best and greatest persons, in their various stations and capacities, should do what they can to encourage and promote true piety in such magistrates in their places, by encouraging schools and colleges and ministers in their places, and by public and private instructions, should strive to promote true piety in young persons.

Needful Instructions

Thirdly, good instructions (or teachings) ordinarily are needful for the fear of God or true practical piety. I will teach you the fear of the Lord. Man needs to be taught the right way, to order his walking in it. Proverbs 19:2 says that *"It is not good for a soul to be without knowledge."* Sound knowledge is needful for a right practice. *"He will teach us His ways, And we shall walk in His paths"* (Mic. 4:2). *"If you know these things, blessed are you if you do them"* (John 13:17). But the doctrine I design chiefly to insist on at present, is this:

Doctrine: That children, or young persons, should make it their chief, principal care and business, to fear God, and to be sincerely and practically pious.

This was the thing that the royal prophet in our text was so solicitous to instill on children, namely, to fear God. As soon as children become capable of acting as rational creatures, by deliberately considering things, by intelligently choosing and refusing, even then (and afterwards forever) they should fear God, and should make it their chief endeavor to please Him, that they may enjoy Him. This truly is the one thing needful. All other matters are baubles and trifles compared to this. Here is the truest wisdom they can manifest: *"The fear of the Lord, that is wisdom, and to depart from evil is understanding"* (Job 28:28). Therefore, people should *"Remember now your Creator in the days of your youth"* (Eccl. 12:1). God gives them great encouragement to do so, in saying, *"I love those who love me, and those who seek me diligently will find me"* (Prov. 8:17).

The Nature of Early Piety

I will now endeavor in some measure to describe the nature of early piety, showing what it is, wherein it does consist, how or wherein it should exert or exemplify itself. Therefore we may inquire,

Question: What is here implied or comprehended, in a child's fearing of God?

Answer: Their fearing of God, according to the sense of our text, may well be comprehended in these following things:

The Attributes of God

1. Their believing of, and meditating on, the being and attributes of God.

The belief of a God of an eternal power and Godhead, of a Being infinitely perfect, that is the Maker and Governor of all things, is the very foundation, the first article of all true religion. He that does not believe there is a God, can neither love nor fear Him. *"But without faith it is impossible to please Him, for he who comes to God must believe that He is, and that He is a rewarder of those who diligently seek Him"* (Heb. 11:6). God is indeed infinite, eternal, unchangeable in His being, wisdom, power, holiness, justice, goodness and truth. He is the Sovereign Maker, preserver, supreme Lord, and governor of all creatures. *"He does according to His will in the army of heaven and among the inhabitants of the earth"* (Dan. 4:35). God has made men for eternity, and they will be eternally happy or miserable, depending upon whether they submit to or rebel against Him, their maker, lawgiver, and judge. It is therefore the indispensible duty, and undeniable interest of all persons, young as well as old, to fear and obey God. A firm belief of such things as these, is necessarily implied in, or absolutely necessary for a right fearing of God.

Children therefore cannot have their thoughts and meditations better employed than on the being and perfections of God. Children are apt to have their meditations run much on empty babbles and vanities, but when they are duly exercised on God and His matchless excellencies, it is the most proper and noble employment they can possibly be engaged in.

The Will of God

2. Their hearty, studious, diligent acquainting of themselves with God's will revealed in His written Word.

How far those utterly unacquainted with the Scriptures are capable of knowing and fearing God, I will not now inquire. But those young ones referred to in our text were the children of the covenant, the children of God's professing people, to whom He gave His word, statutes, and judgments though He has not done so with every nation (Ps. 147:19-20).

If young persons among a professing people would rightly fear God, they should diligently study His will, to direct them in it, and quicken them to it, for His revealed will shows what He forbids, what He requires, and what obligations they are under to obey Him. *"He has shown you, O man, what is good; and what does the Lord require of you but to do justly, to love mercy, and to walk humbly with your God"* (Mic. 6:8)? This He has done in the Holy Scriptures, *"which are able to make you wise for salvation through faith which is in Christ Jesus"* (2 Tim. 3:15). Timothy, in his childhood, knew those Scriptures, and so should others also even while they are children. The Scriptures are God's law. They are Christ's love letter to His people, and they are the saints' charter containing the privileges belonging to them.

Reading the Bible

Children, therefore, should maintain a diligent, constant practice of reading the Holy Scriptures, regarding them as the light of their feet, and lamp of their paths (Ps. 119:105). *"Search the Scriptures"* (John 5:39). Let the Word of Christ dwell in you richly. Meditate on God's law, night and day (Ps. 1:2). Hide it in your hearts, that you may not sin against God. *"How can a young man cleanse his way? By taking heed according to Your word"* (Ps. 119:9). O children, you cannot rightly fear and serve God, unless you are acquainted with His revealed will. You must know His will, else you cannot do it, either what He forbids, that you may avoid it, or what He requires, that you may perform it.

Study

Study to know God's will, both as a part and as a means of that fear you owe to Him. *"Know the God of your father, and serve Him with a loyal heart and with a willing mind; for the LORD searches all hearts and understands all the intent of the thoughts. If you seek Him, He will be found by you; but if you forsake Him, He will cast you off forever"* (1 Chron. 28:9).

Know the God of your fathers, that you may *"prove what is that good and acceptable and perfect will of God"* (Rom. 12:2). *"My people are destroyed for lack of knowledge. Because you have rejected knowledge, I also will reject you from being priest for Me"* (Hosea 4:6).

Again, study God's will, as a means of that fear you owe to Him. To practice His will is the end that should be aimed at in seeking knowledge. We should study to know God's holy will, with a purpose, desire and design to do it and to conform to it. *"This Book of the Law shall not depart from your mouth, but you shall meditate in it day and night, that you may observe to do according to all that is written in it"* (Josh. 1:8).

We are to be *"teaching them to observe all things that I have commanded you"* (Matt. 28:20). The commands of Christ should be taught (and therefore learned) that they may be observed and obeyed.

Prize Your Bible

Therefore, O children, prize your Bible as the best of all books. Prize it above gold, above much fine gold, esteem it sweeter than honey or the honeycomb (Ps. 19:10). It shows you how to get peace with God, how to please Him, how to honor Christ and get honor in His sight; it shows you how to get pardon of sin, how to behave yourselves in every station and condition, how to get a sanctified use of providences, how to save your souls, to escape hell, get to heaven, and possess eternal glory. Let this best of books be the chief subject of your study and meditation. How much time is wretchedly mispent, thrown away, lost, in reading play-books or filthy and profane writings! Seriously and diligently reading and studying the Holy Bible is one good means to make us wise to salvation, holy in temporal life, and happy for eternity.

Our Guilty State

Again, for children to fear God rightly implies the serious consideration of their naturally sinful and guilty state. If young persons seriously read and study God's word, and consider what is contained in it, they cannot help but see, that as they proceed from fallen apostate Adam, they are unspeakably vile, filthy and guilty. They were *"brought forth in iniquity"* and conceived in sin (Ps. 51:5). *"The heart is deceitful above all things, and desperately wicked"* (Jer. 17:9). Their *"carnal mind is enmity against God; for it is not subject to the law of God, nor indeed can be"* (Rom. 8:7). Their hearts naturally, are a mere nest, root, and fountain of sin and wickedness. An evil treasure from whence proceed evil things, that is, evil thoughts, murders, adulteries, etc. (Matt. 12:35; 15:19).

Children of Wrath

Indeed, as sharers in the guilt of Adam's first sin, they are *"by nature children of wrath"* (Eph. 2:3), liable to eternal vengeance, the unquenchable flames of hell.

Hearts Estranged From God

But besides this, their hearts (as has been said) are unspeakably wicked, estranged from God, and at enmity against Him, eagerly set in pursing vanities, and in provoking God by actual personal transgressions, whereby they merit and deserve greater measures of wrath. While they continue in such a state, with sin reigning and tyrannizing in them and guilt lying on them, I say, while they are in this state, they have *"no fear of God before their eyes"* (Rom. 3:18). They have not that fear of God which is acceptable to Him. *"Those who are in the flesh cannot please God"* (Rom. 8:8).

While they are in this state, they can yield no acceptable service to God, nor have they any title to His pardoning mercy, or reconciled favor. It truly behooves them most seriously to consider how filthy, guilty, odious, and abominable they are both by nature and by practice. They should see their sickness, and so their need of a physician; their danger of the pursuing wrath of God, and also their need of refuge (Heb. 6:18).

Turning to God

Their rightly fearing of God implies their turning from sin to God in Christ Jesus. The Lord Jesus Christ, God and man in one person, is the only *"Mediator between God and men"* (1 Tim. 2:5), and the only and all-sufficient Savior of sinners (Acts 4:12). He came to *"save His people from their sins"* and iniquities (Matt. 1:21), to purify them and make them *"zealous for good works"* (Titus 2:14), and to save and deliver them from wrath to come (1 Thess. 1:10).

It is only in and through this blessed Mediator and Redeemer, that sinners can obtain pardon of sin, peace, friendship, and reconciliation with God. God is in Christ, *"reconciling the world to Himself"* (2 Cor. 5:19). God can be *"just and the justifier of the one who has faith in Jesus"* (Rom. 3:26).

The New Birth

Indeed, the Spirit of God must set in, with His Word, and make it efficacious to convince the soul of its sin, guilt, danger, and to draw it to Christ, trusting only in His meritorious righteousness for pardon, peace, and reconciliation with God. Except a man be born again, *"he cannot see the kingdom of God"* (John 3:3).

God must take away the heart of stone, and *"give you a heart of flesh"* (Ezek. 36:26). God must renew persons in the spirit of their minds and grant to them *"the washing of regeneration and renewing of the Holy Spirit"* (Titus 3:5). He will create them in Christ Jesus *"for good works"* (Eph. 2:10) and they must by faith receive Christ else they cannot have peace with God. Being *"justified by faith, we have peace with God through our Lord Jesus Christ"* (Rom. 5:1). *"He who believes in Him is not condemned; but he who does not believe is condemned already, because he has not believed in the name of the only begotten Son of God"* (John 3:18). *"He who believes in the Son has everlasting life; and he who does not believe the Son shall not see life, but the wrath of God abides on him"* (John 3:36).

Regenerating Change

It is absolutely necessary to have a regenerating, converting change wrought in the soul and to have the soul united to Christ by faith. Oh children, that is the one thing most needful and most profitable. Do not think it is enough that you were born of Christian parents, that you were baptized, educated, and instructed in the true Christian religion. Do not think that until now you have appeared to lead blameless religious lives. All these things may possibly be true of many hypocrites. All these things may be true of you, and yet you perish forever.

Repentance

See to it therefore, that you heartily repent of sin and submit to Christ as Prince and Savior. *"Repentance toward God and faith toward our Lord Jesus Christ"* (Acts 20:21) are the great things instilled in the gospel.

The scope of the gospel is to turn men from darkness to light, *"from the power of Satan to God, that they may receive forgiveness of sins and an inheritance among those who are sanctified by faith in Me"* (Acts 28:18). Therefore, do not content yourselves with anything short of a hearty submission to the calls of the gospel. Do not think there will be enough time to mind your souls hereafter; don't indulge yourselves in any vicious carousing or in any ways of known wickedness, thereby provoking God, dishonoring Christ, resisting the Holy Spirit, grieving your pious parents and neighbors, gratifying the devil, and treasuring up wrath against the day of wrath.

Do not be agents for hell, factors for the devil, hastening to and ripening for damnation, but penitently fly to Christ for refuge to save you from sin, guilt, wrath, and misery. Seriously consider with yourselves how contrary your fallen natures are to the holy image and laws of God. Consider how frequently, basely, abominably you have broken the holy laws of the glorious God, that good God who is the author of your beings and all your benefits.

Consider

Consider the terrible eternal wrath and vengeance which your sins have justly deserved and your own utter inability to save yourselves from them, and then be ashamed of them, and loath yourself for all your offences.

Outward Appearance

Young persons are often apt to be very proud, often proud of their fine, gay clothes in which they appear to the view of men. Yet, if they duly considered how dirty, filthy, loathsome, and abominable their sins render them in the sight of the infinitely holy God, this might justly fill them with the greatest shame, grief, sorrow, and self-abhorrence for their sins.

"'*Then you will remember your evil ways and your deeds that were not good; and you will loathe yourselves in your own sight, for your iniquities and your abominations. Not for your sake do I do this,' says the Lord God, 'let it be known to you. Be ashamed and confounded for your own ways'*" (Ezek. 36:31-32).

Receive Him by Faith

Nothing should be so great a grief, load, or burden to you as the sinfulness of your natures and the numberless sinful thoughts, words, and actions that have issued from them. I will be *"in anguish over my sin"* (Ps. 38:18). You should heartily and immovably trust in Jesus Christ for pardon. Indeed, if you do not penitently receive Christ by faith, you are not accepted by God. You have no true fear of God in you. You may have a slavish terrifying fear like the devils who believe and tremble, but a truly obedient fear of God, such as is acceptable to Him, you do not have unless you receive Christ by faith. You must submit to Him as the Prophet, Priest, and King of your souls.

Profitable Duty

This hearty, penitent trusting in and submitting to Christ is a most necessary profitable duty. It should not be delayed but most speedily engaged in. *"Today, if you will hear His voice, do not harden your hearts"* (Heb. 4:7). Those who are not united to Christ by heart-purifying faith, (whatever their outward religious performances and privileges may be), are children of the devil, slaves to their own lusts, enemies to God and Christ, the subjects of guilt, having no pardon of sin nor title to glory, but are condemned by the law and are every moment in danger of dropping into hell.

O, rest not in such a condition, but most speedily and heartily submit to Christ on gospel terms, that it may be well with you forever. As a child's right fear of God implies their receiving Christ on gospel terms, so it implies their having their hearts rightly affected to God and conformed to His prescriptive will. Indeed, it comprehends those two extensive duties, that of loving God with all our heart, and our neighbors as ourselves (Matt. 22:37-39). I shall chiefly confine myself to consider the first of these, that is, first table duties. The second table will be handled by others in their lecture-sermons. Well, if young persons would rightly fear God, their hearts should be duly affected to Him and conformed to its precepts. *"My son, give me your heart"* (Prov. 23:26). They must believe with the heart. Their heart must be right with God and steadfast in His covenant. They must cleave to the Lord with full purpose of heart. With this in mind, I might say:

Love God

They should love God. True love and fear of God always go together (Deut. 10:12). They should love God with all their heart, soul, mind, strength. They should love His law. *"Oh, how love I your law! It is my meditation all the day"* (Ps. 119:97). They should esteem it above gold, above much fine gold, and count it worth more than the honey or honeycomb (Ps. 19:10). They should love His holy Sabbaths, His house, ordinances, and worship (Ps. 27:4, 84:10). They should love His children, for His sake; bearing His image and doing His will (1 John 3:14, 5:1). And they should love His ambassadors and ministers as His officers for their work sake. They should love them and submit to them, as employed by Him to watch for their souls (Heb. 13:17).

Glorify God

They should desire to please and glorify God. They should choose the things that please God (Isa. 56:4). *"Walk worthy of the Lord, fully pleasing Him, being fruitful in every good work"* (Col. 1:10). They should so act, *"not as pleasing men, but God who tests"* their hearts (1 Thess. 2:4). Their desire should be to glorify God with their bodies and spirits and to glorify Him in whatever they eat or drink, or whatsoever they do (1 Cor. 6:20, 10:31). Therefore, they should fear to displease or offend God, in any matter whatsoever, either by omitting what He requires or committing what He forbids. Thus should children (as well as others) do. Obadiah said to Elijah, *"I your servant have feared the Lord from my youth"* (1 Kings 18:12). Abijah, while a child, had in him some good thing towards the Lord God of Israel (1 Kings 14:13). While King Josiah was young, his heart was tender, and he humbled himself before God. He exercised a holy love to Him, and fear of Him (2 Chron. 34:8, 27). When Joseph was young, he feared God, desired to please Him and shun what would offend Him, saying, *"How then can I do this great wickedness, and sin against God?"* (Gen. 39:9). Oh that there were such a heart in all the children of the covenant, that they would fear to offend God, though never so strongly tempted to it. Flee youthful lusts. *"My son, if sinners entice you, do not consent"* (Prov. 1:10).

Be Thankful to God

They should be thankful to God for all His favors to them. *"In everything give thanks; for this is the will of God in Christ Jesus for you"* (1 Thess. 5:18). God is their maker, preserver, only benefactor, the guide of their youth, the giver of every good gift. Therefore they should say, as Psalm 103:2 says: *"Bless the Lord, O my soul, and forget not all His benefits."* They should be thankful for all benefits, especially for those that bear a favorable aspect on their spiritual welfare. They ought to give thanks that they were born under the gospel, in a land of Bibles, ministers, Sabbaths, and ordinances; that they were born of Christian parents, under the wing of the covenant, that they had a Christian education, being brought up in the nurture and admonition of the Lord. They should be thankful, that the Lord Jesus Christ did take hold of their souls (as it were) by parental instructions before they could be tainted with those errors and false notions that the children of heathen, Jews, and Muslims suck in (as it were) with their mothers' milk. Divine goodness in this regard should be gratefully acknowledged. Truly they should be unspeakably thankful for and thank our Lord Jesus Christ for the influences of His Holy Spirit, the restraints of His grace, and for any well-grounded hopes (if such we have) of eternal glory. Oh children, be thankful to God for these things, yea, praise His loading you daily with His benefits.

Be Patient

They should be patient under His chastenings and rebukes. *"Do not despise the chastening of the LORD, nor be discouraged when you are rebuked by Him"* (Heb. 12:5). Do not murmur (1 Cor. 10:10), nor fret; but be *"patient in tribulation"* (Rom. 12:12). Bear the indignation of the Lord because you have sinned against Him. Be still and know that He is God. Be dumb and open not your mouths because He does it. *"We have had human fathers who corrected us, and we paid them respect. Shall we not much more readily be in subjection to the Father of spirits and live"* (Heb. 12:9)? *"It is good for a man to bear the yoke in his youth"* (Lam. 3:27).

Doubtless multitudes of young people have had much spiritual advantage by their afflictions. Has not much sin been prevented, their corrupt inclinations greatly checked and restrained by the trials they have met with? May not many of them say, *"Before I was afflicted I went astray, but now I keep Your word"* (Ps. 119:67). *"It is good for me that I have been afflicted, that I may learn Your statutes"* (Ps. 119:71). *"I know, O LORD, that Your judgments are right, and that in faithfulness You have afflicted me"* (Ps. 119:75). Be patient, therefore, under trials.

Submit

They should submit and resign themselves to God's providential disposition. God's providence governs the world. They should consider and regard it in all they meet with, and be willing that He should deal with them as He pleases, learning in whatever state they are in to be content (Philippians 4:11). They should say, *"The will of the Lord be done"* (Acts 21:14). *"It is the LORD. Let Him do what seems good to Him"* (1 Sam. 3:18). *"Here I am, let Him do to me as seems good to Him"* (2 Sam. 15:26). They should say to God, after the example of our Holy Redeemer: *"Nevertheless, not as I will, but as You will"* (Matt. 26:39).

Grieve Over Sin

They should grieve for, and hate those things that are hateful and provoking to God. They should hate all sin in themselves and others and hate even *"every false way"* (Ps. 119:128). They should hate the works of them that turn aside and hate vain thoughts. They should hate sin with a perfect hatred, and that because it is hateful to God. They should grieve and mourn for their own sins and for the sins of others. *"I see the treacherous, and am disgusted, because they do not keep Your word"* (Ps. 119:158). Oh children, you should grieve for your own sinful thoughts, words, and actions and for the wicked words and actions you hear and see in others. Do you hear other children speak profanely, curse and swear, or speak obscene, filthy words? Do they call wicked names, tell lies, behave themselves viciously on any account? Well, do not imitate these things, but mourn for them because they provoke God and wrong the souls of the guilty.

Christ As Their Portion

They should choose, trust, and delight in God and in Christ as their portion *"'The Lord is my portion,' says my soul, 'Therefore I hope in Him'"* (Lam. 3:24). *"For You are my hope, O Lord GOD; You are my trust from my youth"* (Ps. 71:5) They should *"Trust in the Lord forever"* (Isa. 26:4), cast all their cares and burdens upon Him, and commit the keeping of their souls unto Him. They should delight themselves in the Lord, count Him to be their exceeding joy, and rejoice in Him always (Ps. 37:4; 43:4; Phil. 4:4). They should prize the light of God's countenance above corn and wine (Ps. 4:6-7). And *"Though the flock may be cut off from the fold, and there be no herd in the stalls— Yet I will rejoice in the Lord, I will joy in the God of my salvation"* (Hab. 3:17-18). Oh children, if you have God in Christ for your portion, it is an unspeakably greater benefit and blessing than to have rich parents, fine clothes, great estates, or any outward temporary enjoyment whatsoever. O, long after and trust in God! *"Whom have I in heaven but You? And there is none upon earth that I desire besides You. My flesh and my heart fail; but God is the strength of my heart and my portion forever"* (Ps. 73:25-26).

Hearts Employed for God

A child's fear of God implies their having their hearts rightly affected to Him and conformed to His precepts. It also implies their sincere, fervent, constant endeavors, that their whole outward carriage and behavior may be agreeable to God's will and pleasing in His sight. Their mouths, hands, and hearts should be employed for God. With their bodies as well as their spirits, they should *"glorify God"* (1 Cor. 6:20). If their hearts are right with God, renewed and sanctified, then, from this good treasure within they will bring forth *"good things"* (Matt. 12:35). Indeed, they should yield universal obedience to God's commands and have respect to them all. *"Obey My voice, and do according to all that I command you; so shall you be My people, and I will be your God"* (Jer. 11:4).

Secret Prayer

Inasmuch as I am to speak chiefly of first table duties, I will under this heading particularly say to children or young people, that they should pray to God in secret. *"Go into your room, and when you have shut your door, pray to your Father who is in the secret place; and your Father who sees in secret will reward you openly"* (Matt. 6:6). *"Seek the Lord while He may be found, call upon Him while He is near"* (Isa. 55:6). Children should, very early on in their lives, pray to God in secret and should maintain a steady course of so praying as long as they live. Morning and evening they should pray alone, pour out their souls to God, confess their sins to Him, pray that He would pardon their sins for Christ's sake, and that He would fill them with His Spirit, with heavenly wisdom and grace. They should pray to the God of their fathers, for all the blessings they need. *"Give Your strength to Your servant, and save the son of Your maidservant"* (Ps. 86:16). They should pray for more knowledge (Ps. 119:18), wisdom (James 1:5.), and for unwearied supplies of grace that they may shun wickedness and practice holiness (Ps. 19:13-14; 25:4-5). They should pray for all the blessings they need, both for body and soul, for time and for eternity, and as they ought to pray for themselves, so they should for others too. *"Pray one for another"* (James 5:16). Oh children, be not so vile and wicked, as to live without secret prayer! Do not let a morning or evening pass, without getting alone for this most profitable, reasonable service.

Remember the Sabbath Day

They should remember the Sabbath day to keep it holy. *"You shall keep My Sabbaths and reverence My sanctuary"* (Lev. 19:30). Oh children, do not profane God's Sabbath by idleness, playing, and needless speaking about worldly matters, much less by anything in itself sinful, but employ the Sabbath in praying, reading the Holy Bible and good books, learning your catechism, receiving the good instructions of parents and masters in going to the house of God, and diligently and reverently attending His holy worship. *"If you turn away your foot from the Sabbath, from doing your pleasure on My holy day, and call the Sabbath a delight, The holy day of the LORD honorable, and shall honor Him, not doing your own ways, nor finding your own pleasure, nor speaking your own words"* (Isa. 58:13).

Wait on God

They should wait on God in all His ordinances, and therefore seriously and devoutly come to the Lord's Supper. They should not forsake the assembling of themselves together (Heb. 10:25), but reverence God's sanctuary (Lev. 19:30). They should love the habitation of His house, and the place where His honor dwells (Ps. 26:8), accounting one day in His courts better than a thousand, (Ps. 84:10), desiring to *"dwell in the house of the Lord"* all the days of their lives, to *"behold the beauty of the Lord, and to inquire in His temple"* (Ps. 27:4). They should have earnest honoring and pursuing after God in His ordinances (Ps. 42:1-2), and to see His power and His glory in His sanctuary (Ps. 63:2). Indeed, they should walk in all the ordinances and commandments of the Lord blameless (Luke 1:6). Therefore, they should heartily and seriously wait on the Lord in the ordinance of His Supper.

They should examine themselves, eat of that bread and drink of that cup, and should do it in remembrance of Christ, to show forth His death, till He comes. They should seriously consider the author, nature, end, and use of this ordinance, and should come to it out of love and obedience to Christ - to promote His glory and their own spiritual good. They should renew and seal the covenant dedication of themselves to Him in this holy institution. Indeed, they should not dare to neglect this ordinance. By neglecting it, they disobey God, dishonor Christ, grieve the Holy Spirit, gratify the devil, set a bad example before men, and wrong their own souls. How dare they bring the guilt of these things upon themselves?

Thus, I have given a few general hints, showing what is implied in children's and young ones' fearing of God, or being practically pious.

Lament for Apostasy

It is a matter of lamentation that there is no more of this fear of God appearing in the children and the young persons among this people. It is to be hoped indeed, that there are many children and young persons among this people who remember their Creator, who fear the Lord in their youth, and give comfortable evidences of their sincere piety. Yet, it is a matter of great lamentation that there are no more such. Are there not many young persons who show little if any regard to God, to Christ, and to the welfare of their precious immortal souls? Are there not many young ones who seldom, if ever, read God's Holy Word, unless (as it were), constrained or compelled to it and who scarce learn, or soon forget, their catechism of such sound words?

Many who give little, if any reason to think that they should retire morning and evening for secret prayer? Many who show little, if any regard to God's holy Sabbath, but rather profane it by playing, idleness, worldly and vain discourses, and neglecting private and public exercises of religious worship? Alas, how many are there who evidently disregard their baptismal dedication to God? In baptism they have been solemnly dedicated, consecrated to the service of God, and are obliged with body and soul to glorify God the Father, God the Son, and God the Holy Spirit. Yet, when they are grown up, do they not seem practically to renounce the God of their fathers, to cast off the hope of their fathers, and to employ their bodies and souls in the service of the devil and their own lusts and corruptions?

Nay, are there not some young persons, children of the covenant, baptized ones, that are very ignorant of christianity? Some will take God's holy name in vain and will curse and swear profanely. Such are guilty of horrid sacrilege. They rob God. They employ in the service of Satan and the gratifying their own corruptions. Surely such things as these ought to be deeply lamented. All that have at heart the cause of God, the honor of Christ, and the good of this people, should bewail what is amiss among us, and pray for the outpouring of God's spirit for the mending and reforming of it.

Humility for Past Sins

Those of us who have passed through the time of our youth should be humbled for the sins then committed. Was not much of our childhood and youth, spent in vanity? If we seriously reflect and look back, might we call to mind that we were very unmindful of God, of Christ, and of the concerns of our souls, that we did not so early, steadily, constantly read God's word, pray in secret, and devoutly attend His public worship as we should have done? How little good did we get, how little good did we do, and how much guilt did we contract in our younger days? Indeed, so far as we were restrained and influenced by the Word and Spirit of God, we should bless Him for it. Yet, have we no great reason to be deeply humbled and self-abased, that we were not more early, hearty, servent, diligent, and constant in seeking and serving God? If we had been duly studious, diligent, constant in duty, how much greater progress might we have made in holy knowledge and practical piety?

How much reason have we to pray, as Psalm 25:7 says, *"Do not remember the sins of my youth, nor my transgressions; According to Your mercy remember me, For Your goodness' sake, O Lord."*

Promotion of True Piety

All that are concerned with children, with young persons, should strive to encourage and promote true piety in them. Parents should do so, masters and mistresses in families, and in schools, should do so. Ministers should do so, feeding the lambs as well as the sheep of Christ's flock. *"Godliness is profitable for all things"* (1 Tim. 4:8). Everybody, in their several stations and capacities in life, should encourage and promote what is so profitable. Nothing is more threatening to the welfare of a people than to have their young ones generally ignorant, irreligious, and disorderly. When it is so, it looks as though iniquity would soon abound, to the pulling down heavy judgments.

Hope for the Future

So, nothing looks more promising than to have their young ones generally fearing and serving God. *"Righteousness exalts a nation, but sin is a reproach to any people"* (Prov. 14:34). All proper methods therefore should be taken to promote true piety in young persons.

"For He established a testimony in Jacob, and appointed a law in Israel, which He commanded our fathers, that they should make them known to their children; that the generation to come might know them, the children who would be born, that they may arise and declare them to their children, that they may set their hope in God, and not forget the works of God, but keep His commandments" (Ps. 78:5-7).

Unspeakable Profit

When true practical religion is thus propagated among a people from one generation to another, it will be unspeakably profitable and advantageous to them.

"The mercy of the Lord is from everlasting to everlasting on those who fear Him, and His righteousness to children's children, to such as keep His covenant, and to those who remember His commandments to do them" (Ps. 103:17-18).

"Let the peoples praise You, O God; Let all the peoples praise You. Then the earth shall yield her increase; God, our own God, shall bless us. God shall bless us, And all the ends of the earth shall fear Him" (Ps. 67:5-7).

3

EARLY PIETY & RESPECTING AUTHORITY

Mr. Colman, Boston, April 6, 1721

Ephesians 6:2
"Honor your father and mother," which is the first commandment with promise.

In the last lecture, the nature of early piety was stated and explained as it respects the glorious God. The duty of young people toward him their Creator and Redeemer was laid before them. That which follows next in order and which therefore falls to me, is to speak of the nature of early piety as it respects men. Tihat is to say, the duty incumbent upon young people, by the law and commandment of God their Savior, to men in the various relations wherein they stand to them. To this end, I have chosen these words of the apostle, which repeat the first part of the Fifth Commandment, *"Honor thy father and mother,"* and refer to the latter part of it that states it is the first commandment with promise.

We have here a precept and commandment directed to young people, and provide reasons to recommend it to them and enforce it on them.

A Broad Precept

The precept, the same which was given from the beginning at the delivery of the law from Sinai and He who then spoke it by angels in thunders from the burning mountains, now speaks it to you, O our children, from the mouth of His apostle (the apostle of the Gentiles) another angel of His church. And this is not to you only, but to the whole assembly who are included with you in this law that is exceedingly broad.

Therefore, we hope that you will attend with great fear and reverence, as the parents with their children in the congregation of Israel did, when these words were first spoken from heaven. In the name of that great God whose voice then shook the earth, and the trembling people prayed that they might no longer hear it as they then did, lest they should die under the fright, in the name of this great God. I bring this part of His law to you this day: honor thy father and mother.

A Precept for All

The precept in my text not only speaks to children, but is immediately directed to them. For so the chapter begins, *"Children, obey your parents in the Lord, for this is right. Honor your father and mother"* (Eph. 6:1-2).

Had I taken these words out of the commandment itself, as it lies in the 20th chapter of Exodus, they would have been meant and directed as well to parents and masters, magistrates and ministers, as unto children, but here, they are spoken and meant for you children and young people, in your age of government and subjection.

Honor Toward Parents

But by father and mother you are to understand it as referring to your proper parents, your natural father who begat you, and your mother who bore you, and also those that may stand in the place of parents to you, to whose care and government you may be committed if you are orphans, or by whom you may be adopted, or being destitute and helpless may be cast upon by the providence of God.

Honor Toward All Superiors

Moreover, though the text here means and limits the precept strictly to children and the father and mother spoken of are the natural or legal parents, for masters and servants are afterward spoken to by themselves, yet I will take leave to speak of father and mother here in the same latitude and extent as the Fifth Commandment in the Decalogue is ever to be interpreted. So, by *"father"* and *"mother,"* I mean all your superiors in family, school, church and commonwealth, yea, every relative you have in the world. Your equals or your inferiors are to come into consideration with you, and the honor here required of you takes in the whole duty which God requires of you in every relation wherein you stand toward men. So great and broad is the commandment before you.

Command

This is the first commandment with promise. The Fifth Commandment in the Decalogue has this singular and distinguishing thing in it, which the Holy Spirit thinks worthy of special remark. It is the first precept in the second table of the law and has a promise added to enforce it, which none of the following commandments have. Thus, it is the first, even the only commandment of the ten with a particular promise (the promise of a particular mercy). In the Second Commandment we find a general promise of mercy made, but in the Fifth Commandment there is a particular mercy specified, namely, a long and happy life on the earth.

The Mercy of the Command

The mercy promised in the Second Commandment is to all that keep the commandments in general; that mercy promised in the Fifth Commandment is unto them that keep this commandment. This is eminently the commandment with promise, having a special promise attached to the particular duty commanded. The promise attached to the Second Commandment is a general one which relates to the whole law, but this is a special one which respects this commandment in particular.

Now children, God prescribes to you a special regard unto this His commandment, which contains in it the piety which you are to discharge towards men. You must consider it as a prime and special precept of His law. You must discharge the duties which are prescribed in it in obedience unto the great God, whose commandment it is. You must eye His authority and act for His glory in doing your duty to your parents, your superiors, inferiors, and equals. You must eye the promise to which He has attached to this commandment, that you may obtain His favor and blessing.

Wherefore children, mind it, both the precept and the promise from a pious heart and mind, from a principle of grace within you, in a religious manner and for holy ends. For the honor of God and for your own eternal salvation, you observe these duties which are this day preached to you from these words.

For the Love of God

Observe, therefore, that piety toward God is presupposed, and to be laid in the foundation of these moral duties which God sends me now to require of you, or else, though you carry yourselves laudably toward your parents at home, and in the sight of all men abroad. Yet you will be no examples of early piety, for though you could say to me when I have finished, as the young man in the gospel said to our Savior, *"All these things I have kept from my youth"* (Matthew 19:20), yet it must be said to you again, one thing you lack: you do it not from the fear and love of God in your soul, but from a principle of grace and piety within you.

I call upon you therefore, children, to remember how you were taught the fear of the Lord in the last lecture day, and in that fear of God now, to hearken to me and set yourselves by the help of God's grace to observe and do the things that are now to be commanded you by God. Instead of the promised blessing, you will find the divine threats and curses which are implied in the promise executed upon you. If not in this life yet, in that which is to come (which is infinitely worse).

The Reward

Let me here hint at one more thing to you children. You may, and should in your obedience to God, consider the promise and reward of God, even unto a present and temporal reward of your piety toward men. It has the promise of the life that it may be well with you, and that you may live long upon the earth as are the words after my text. You must eye the commandment of God in the first place. Obey your parents in the Lord, because He commands it, and in all things that are agreeable to His will, because this is right and just, by the law of nature and nations as well as by the written word. Then you may consider the recompense of reward.

Honor Expressed Outwardly

Having thus opened the text unto you a little, in such a manner as to awaken your attention, and if it might be to touch your tender hearts. I now come to declare to you (our children) how true piety ought to be operating in your souls, and how it ought to be expressed in your words, actions, and behavior toward men. In this you are always to exercise yourselves that you may keep a conscience void of offence toward God.

Now the best and plainest method, as well as fullest manner, wherein I may lay your duty before you, is, I think, in these four headings in which our Boston-Catechism, or milk for babes has long since given it: family, school, church and commonwealth.

Honor in the Family

Early piety will show itself in the religious carriage of children and young people in the families they are a part of and in a conscientious discharge of the particular duties which they owe (by the law of God) unto one and another in the family. For instance, you are a child of the family, or in it, and must show piety to your parents or those that are instead of father and mother to you. You are a brother or a sister in the family, and have brothers and sisters to show piety unto. There are workers for your family, and there is a piety to be expressed to them, or you are a worker in a family and there is piety to be expressed by them toward all in the house.

You are a child of the family, born in it, and your first and earliest piety must be expressed to your parents or those that are in the stead of father and mother to you. This relation and so this duty stands first in the order of nature, for next to your duty to God, your heavenly Father is that which you owe to your earthly parents. Your father and mother are next to and immediately under God, the instrumental authors of your being. You are the children that God has given to them. Theirs is the propriety in you as soon as you are born, and they have the first dominion and most rightful government over you, and an absolute one for your good in your infancy, you being altogether incapable of acting for yourself.

And then God has implanted in your parents that tender and unspeakable love, desire, care and solicitude for your good. From the day when you were born, they have been expressing it towards you in such ways and with such pleasure, as to oblige and bind you to render our very selves to them, and all the reverence, honor, gratitude, and affection of your souls, in subordination to God and the honor and obedience which you owe to Him.

Honor Toward God

See how God has joined piety to parents with piety toward Himself. *"Every one of you shall revere his mother and his father, and keep My Sabbaths: I am the Lord your God"* (Lev. 19:3).

Children, let me tell you, you cannot fear and worship God if you do not fear your father and your mother. Your father in heaven will accept no worship from you, if you do not at the same time carry yourselves piously toward your earthly parents. And mind, as your mother is named in the commandment along with your father, and as in the place not now quoted, the mother is first named and then the father, so before God means especially to admonish you to honor and fear your good mothers, whom you are most likely to ignore and be in danger to set light by, but to whom you are no less bound and obligated than to your father. Your mothers will teach you, as by precept; so, by their own reverence and subjection to your fathers, your first regards are to their will and commands.

Love Them as the Lord

Children! Your duty to your parents is so large and copious a subject that I can but hint at the particulars contained in it. You must love them, next to God, with all your souls, as they do you. The inward esteem of your souls must be upon all occasions expressed in all your words to them and of them in all your actions and whole behavior before them. Your whole carriage must be full of high reverence toward them. Even if you become governors and kings, you must continue this, like Joseph, who bowed himself with his face to the earth when he brought his sons out from between Jacob's knees, and like Solomon, when he rose up from his throne to meet his mother and bowed himself unto her. The illustrious examples are recorded for your admonition and imitation.

Obedience to Parents

Moreover, piety requires that this reverence to your parents be shown by most ready obedience to all their lawful commands. *"Children obey your parents in all things, for this is well pleasing to the Lord"* (Col. 3:20). That is, says one, *"Come when they call you, go where they send you, do what that they bid you, do not do what they forbid you, and do it all from a principle of love. Do this in the fear of God."*

"The eye that mocks his father, And scorns obedience to his mother, The ravens of the valley will pick it out, And the young eagles will eat it" (Prov. 30:17). Let that child fear, lest he perish by the judgments of God and come to the gallows, or some disastrous end.

Learning from Parents

To obey, you must be diligent and reverently learn from your wise and good parents who will be careful to instruct you. Believe, receive, and retain their words. *"My son, hear the instruction of your father, And do not forsake the law of your mother"* (Prov. 1:8). Solomon piously remembered and recorded the good doctrine and institutions of his pious parents. *"I was my father's son, Tender and the only one in the sight of my mother, He also taught me, and said to me: 'Let your heart retain my words; Keep my commands, and live'"* (Prov. 4:2-4).

It will be your piety, O our young people, to regard solemnly the way of worship which you have been instituted from the Word of God. Take heed to yourself and keep your soul diligently and cleave to the God of your father and to His ordinances, lest you forget them and lest they depart from your heart all the days of your life. Teach them to your sons, and your grandsons.

Parents Instruction

Once more, piety requires your reverent submission to the instructions, admonitions, rebukes, and corrections of your parents. To refuse to obey is rebellion against God and His authority with which He has invested in all parents, one which parents can no more put off than they can (or may), natural affection. *"He who spares his rod hates his son"* (Prov. 13:24). You know what God has declared the reward of the rebellious son to be, that he is detestable to Him and to men (Deut. 21:20).

Imitating Faithful Parents

Again, piety requires children to imitate their parents in what is good and exemplary in them and in that only. Let their virtuous and godly lives be a living law to you and be held in great veneration by you, as long as you live. But carefully cover what is amiss in them, as becomes the children of Japheth whom God hath enlarged, and to whom was reckoned for piety that he went backwards and drew a covering over his father's nakedness (Gen. 9:23). Moreover, piety requires of children that they be just and faithful to their parents' outward estate; that they never take of it but what is given to them, nor waste it but rather help and serve it if they can. A child may not steal from his father, as he that mistreats him is a son that *"causes shame and brings reproach"* (Prov. 19:26).

Care of Parents

Another great branch of filial piety is to requite and recompense your parents according to your ability when you are grown up, for all of their kindness and goodness to you. This is the law of God unto you. Toward them, learn to show piety at home and to requite their parents for that is *"good and acceptable before God"* (1 Tim. 5:4).

Helping Parents

But how can children ever requite their parents? Children may, by being wise and pious, offer an ample reward (Prov. 23:15-16). Thy father and thy mother shall be glad and they that bear you shall rejoice. They may requite their parents by defending their parents' person, name, or memory. They *"shall speak with their enemies in the gate"* (Ps. 127:5). Children may also requite their parents by ministering to them in sickness, in weaknesses, and in age, with pleasure, tending those who first tended them. As years and infirmities grow on your parents, let your tender and reverent regards grow toward them, remembering how in your helpless age they pitied and regarded you.

It is the commandment of God to you, *"Do not despise your mother when she is old"* (Prov. 23:22). Vile and impious is the youth that does. *"'Cursed is the one who treats his father or his mother with contempt.' And all the people shall say, 'Amen!'"* (Deut. 27:16). He perishes under a universal curse. All must consent and agree in it.

Finally, piety will teach you to requite your parents by contributing cheerfully to their sustenance and support out of your estate if they stand in need of it. Read Joseph's filial piety in Genesis 45:9-11: *"Hurry and go up to my father, and say to him, 'Thus says your son Joseph: "God has made me lord of all Egypt; come down to me, do not tarry. You shall dwell in the land of Goshen, and you shall be near to me, you and your children, your children's children, your flocks and your herds, and all that you have. There I will provide for you, lest you and your household, and all that you have, come to poverty."'"*

Christ teaches you in Matthew 15:4 that the honoring of your father and mother includes maintenance and relief and He vehemently condemns the false gloss or tradition of the Pharisees that taught otherwise. O child, desire to be unto your parents another Obed, of whom we read, *"He shall be to thee 'a restorer of life and a nourisher of your old age'"* (Ruth 4:15).

Prayer for Parents

Once more, piety will teach children to pray for their parents and to thank God for the blessing they have in them. Piety will teach children to reverently rise up and call them blessed and to desire their blessing, prize their prayers, and see that their soul may bless them. You cannot value the blessing of pious parents at too high of a rate, nor are any pains too great to obtain it, as Joseph went with his two sons to Jacob's knees, with utmost reverence and joy.

But fear a parent's curse! Micah had more religion than to make light of this. He restored the eleven hundred shekels of silver about which his mother cursed. Pious Jacob trembled at the thought of Isaac's curse. Whether he took it to heart we know not, but the story is dreadful to read in Genesis 9: *"Cursed be Canaan; A servant of servants he shall be to his brethren. And he said: 'Blessed be the Lord, the God of Shem, and may Canaan be his servant.'"*

Honoring Advice

I will only add here that piety will teach children to have a just regard for the wisdom and advice of parents. In the disposing of themselves to callings, into families, into marriage, or when God takes parents away, piety requires their children to mourn for them and over them, as Joseph *"fell on his father's face, and wept over him, and kissed him"* as soon as he gave up the ghost (Gen. 50:1).

The Foundation of All Other Relationships

But enough of the piety of children to parents, on which I have enlarged more than any other heading, because it is indeed the first and greatest branch of early piety toward men and is to be laid in the foundation of all the following instances. I will only recommend it further from the example of Christ, the most blessed and glorious lantern of it.

Christ's Honor Toward His Mother

Children, when the Son of God took our nature of the blessed virgin Mary, we read of Him that He was *"subject"* to His parents (Luke 2:51). And as He hung on the cross, He cast down a dying look upon His mother, and said to the beloved disciple who stood by her, *"Behold your mother"* (John 19:27).

John understood the meaning of that gracious endearing word and from that hour, *"took her to his own home"* (John 19:27). Thus Christ being made of a woman was made under the law of the Fifth Commandment, to teach the seed of the faithful to approve themselves unto Him a faithful seed by their careful observance of this commandment. David was a type of Christ in this, that in the day of his distress, he took care of his exposed parents and found a shelter for them (1 Sam. 22:3).

Christ's Honor Toward His Father

But how glorious was the filial piety and dying love of the Son of David, who, when He was suffering under the weight of His eternal Father's frowns, and crying out to Him, *"My God, My God, why have You forsaken Me"* (Matt. 27:46)?

Yet, Christ found a heart and leisure to look down upon His poor pierced mother's soul, and provide her a son and a home.

Imitate Your Savior

O children, imitate your Savior in filial piety. And you that are parents, exact, require, and constrain this duty, fear, and reverence from your children toward you, or you will cruelly abandon them to a reprobate state. It is awful, as both parents and children, to think that among the sins for which God gave up the heathen to a reprobate mind this is one: *"disobedient to parents"* (Rom. 1:30).

Sibling Honor

You are a brother or a sister in the family (we will suppose) and have brothers and sisters to show piety unto. They are thy companions and equals, and next to parents in blood and in the bonds of nature. Here, both God and your parents require you to bestow your next love. Be not like Cain, who was of the Devil and slew his brother, but love as brothers, heartily and fervently, with utmost endearment. Be meek, kind, and obliging in your carriage toward one another. Let not anger rise and rest in your heart, nor passion rage in your looks, in your words, or in your actions one against another. The Devil, not God, (not Christ the Lord God, not the Holy Spirit) dwells in that heart and house where children quarrel, give hard and ill words, call names, wish evil, or fight and strike. Tremble at Christ's words, *"Whoever says, 'You fool!' shall be in danger of hell fire"* (Matt. 5:22).

Bearing With One Another

Bear one with another, bear much (if much must be) one from another. Be silent, suffer wrong, answer not again, and turn the other cheek, for it is your brother. Yet reprove him, more gently or severely, as fits the occasion. Tell him of the fault and sin in what he says or does, and if he will not hear you, inform your parents of his evil manners. Bring them the report of his evil deeds as Joseph did to Jacob concerning his brothers. Though you may be hated by him for it, God will love you. Be sure that you be always true to one another and just. Do not falsely accuse, lie, or deny when you are justly accused.

Pray For Your Brother

Finally, children, pray for one another, for why should not the children of the same house pray with one another, and teach one another? Show to each other a reverence and fear of God in all your conversation together. Encourage each other to fear God, pray to Him, and avoid sin. Especially let each other see that you love and honor the Holy Bible, God's holy Sabbaths, His ministers, and His worshipers. And let the governors of families teach, require, and lead the children into this pious behavior, one toward another.

Honor Toward Workers

If there are workers in your family, you must be very good and pious toward them. Likewise, if you are a worker in a family, there is a piety to be expressed by you toward all that are in the house. An ingenious worker is like a child in a family and should be treated as one. The son during childhood is like a servant though he is heir of all. The children of the house must not be suffered to be imperious, insolent, and tyrannical toward the lowest worker therein and much less toward the superior workers to whom it may, at times and in many cases, belong to direct and overrule the children for their good, and for the good order of the household.

Honor Toward Authority

Abraham's servant was a kind of son to his master and a kind of father to Isaac. Had he begat him, he could not have spoken nor done more for him than he did. Such a servant, if an equal in years, should be regarded by children as a kind of brother, or, if their elder, to take care of them as a kind of under parent.

Workers in a family must show piety, first to their master and mistress and also to others within the household. To your master and mistress, your duty is given in our context. In words, show the piety and religion that is to govern you in all of your service. *"Bondservants, be obedient to those who are your masters according to the flesh, with fear and trembling, in sincerity of heart, as to Christ; not with eye service, as men-pleasers, but as bondservants of Christ, doing the will of God from the heart, with goodwill doing service, as to the Lord, and not to men"* (Eph. 6:5-7).

How is the precept pressed on you by being thus doubled? You will serve, knowing that whatsoever good thing any man doth, the same will he receive from the Lord, whether he be bond or free. It is the commandment with promise you see to servants, and a greater promise than of the case that now is.

You see (you young people who are workers) that God, your great Master in heaven, demands and exacts piety in you toward Him. From this heavenly principle you honor your masters. *"Let as many bondservants as are under the yoke count their own masters worthy of all honor, so that the name of God and His doctrine may not be blasphemed"* (1 Tim. 6:1). Also God commands that you fear them and be subject to them, though they be not so pious and good to you as they should be. *"Servants, be submissive to your masters with all fear, not only to the good and gentle, but also to the harsh. For this is commendable, if because of conscience toward God one endures grief, suffering wrongfully"* (1 Pet. 2:18-19). O, glorious piety is prescribed to you in this truly divine precept. So serve and shine in the families where you are. Be diligent, mind your business, redeem your time, use your best skill and strength, study to please, and study your masters' interest every way you can. Show all good fidelity and *"adorn the doctrine of God your Savior of all things"* (Titus 2:10). Be true and speak the truth; fear a lie, and loath it, as you would Gehazi's leprosy. Preserve your masters' credit and reputation as far as in you it lies, and keep his trust and secrets.

Submission

Be submissive, humble, silent, not answering again. Keep good order of the house, and especially good hours. Submit to reproof and correction. If you are reproved for your faults, take it thankfully as well as patiently, and if wrongfully, endure the grief, *"knowing that from the Lord you will receive the reward of the inheritance; for you serve the Lord Christ"* (Col. 2:20). Joseph, when he was a servant, was faithful and a blessing, and then suffered meekly for his fidelity, gratitude to man, and for his piety toward God (Gen. 39:8-9).

Honor Toward Fellow Workers

To your fellow-workers, one ought to be loving, kind, courteous, obliging, grateful, meek, gentle, and peaceable. Study to be quiet and to do your own business. Assist one another, bear with one another, give good words, and give a good example. Speak to one another of the things of God, admonish one another, submit one to another, and be clothed with humility. Pray one for another, as God has brought you together under one roof. And so dwell together as the workers of God and heirs together of the grace of life. O what blessings would a family of such workers be one to the other!

Honor Toward Teachers

From the family, let us pass to your teacher. And here children, consider it is your parents that give you teachers, and it is their love and affection to you, their care and concern for you, both for your temporal and eternal good that makes them do it. They do it in duty to God, that you may be an instructed seed to serve Him. They do it in duty to the public that you may be blessings in your generation. They could not answer to God or man, nor to their own hearts, which love you and fear God, to leave you in your natural ignorance and rudeness.

They would be cruel, unnatural, and barbarous to you, as well as irreligious toward God not to be thoughtful for your instruction. Therefore, they put you under the care of virtuous, prudent, and accomplished persons to form you aright in mind and in manners, under the blessing of God upon their great pains which they daily take with you and your minds to useful knowledge. The soul without knowledge is not good.

Now children, you ought to be very sensible of the great benefit you have, thankful to God and man for the early means of instruction which you enjoy, and be told that your advantage and happiness in this respect is peculiar among the English provinces. Your wise and pious ancestors made it their first and chief care to have religion and learning flourish among their posterity, to which end as they put themselves under the watch of learned and holy pastors.

This day therefore, we call upon you, our children and young people, to religiously and diligently improve the means of education which you are blessed with. God expects it of you, your parents command it, your ministers charge you, and you are wicked before God if you are idle and negligent at school. *"Wisdom is the principal thing; Therefore get wisdom. And in all your getting, get understanding. Exalt her, and she will promote you; She will bring you honor, when you embrace her. She will place on your head an ornament of grace; A crown of glory she will deliver to you"* (Prov. 4:7-9).

But if you are idle before your teachers you deceive your parents, you are base and ungrateful to them. You do in effect lie to them from day to day. You say, *"Sir, I go to learn, but do not."* You disobey them and rebel against them. Nay, you in effect rob them and steal from them, defraud and cheat them. In all this wickedness you daily live. Is it not the way to be cursed, children?

I will only add, that you must love and esteem, honor and fear, obey and submit to your masters and mistresses who instruct you in the same manner as you would to your father and mother at home. It has been sometimes asked, to which one do you owe the most? To his father for his being, or to his tutor for his institution? But there is no question to be made of this truth. The same piety which a child ought to show to the one at home, he ought to the other at school. With a pious reverence next to that, you remember your parents, remember always your wise and learned and faithful tutors.

The great apostle gratefully speaks of his being brought up at the feet of Gamaliel, from which our children should learn to sit with humility at the feet of them that instruct them, and to mention their names with honor as long as they live. God commands your pious veneration toward them, whom He has adorned, endowed, qualified, and called to teach you. And let all that are so honored to be teachers of children and youth, use their authority over them, and their interest in them, to form them (by the grace of God) unto early piety and religion.

But then you have your fellow students, and piety obliged you not to hinder them in learning or tempt them to play and idleness, but rather to put them on minding their books if they need it to help them in learning it, if they be diligent to be admonished by their example, or if they can inform you to ask of them. And if you would be kind, humble, meek, and grateful one toward another as the dear children of God, walk in peace and love.

Honor Toward Ministers

First, if there be any piety in you it will influence your hearts and appear in your behavior toward the ministers of Christ. They are fathers by office, not only to you but also to your fathers. Your pious parents do themselves entreat them as such, and require you to do so, for the relation they stand in to God and His worship, and to esteem them highly for their works' sake.

Your ministers owe and have a special regard and respect to you, the children, and the young people of their flocks. You are the lambs of whom Christ has said unto us, *"Feed my sheep"* (John 21:17). Your faithful pastors are therefore tenderly concerned for your souls and zealously affected toward you, travelling from birth till Christ be formed in you, till you are newborn. Therefore, you owe it both to God and your pastors, that you love and reverence their persons and their office. If you honor and fear God, or regard your own salvation you will do so.

You must consider them as ministers of Christ and stewards of the mysteries of God, and when you see them say to yourselves, *"These are the servants of the most high God which show us the way of salvation."* You must remember that they have rule over you in the Lord and to submit yourselves to them, for they watch for your souls. You must hearken to them in public and in private, in God's house and in your fathers' houses. When they speak to you the Word of God, believe them fully and perfectly, and lay up their words in your hearts. Desire their prayers. Form yourselves by their grave and gracious conversation.

Give Thanks for Them

Pray for them. Thank God for them, observing that they naturally care for your souls, and that they have no greater joy than to see you walking in the truth. Do not easily believe evil of them. Abhor the act of those that would insinuate into you vile things respecting them, to spoil your reverence of them, and spoil your profits from their ministry. Rebuke and avoid them that would teach you to mock at and revile them. Remember the fate of the forty-two children that perished in such an action (2 Kings 2:24).

Let us see that you reverence God's Sabbaths, fear His Word, and love His ordinances, never daring to trifle and play while your ministers and parents are praying to God and God is speaking to us and you, lest you mourn as the lost and say, *"How have I hated instruction, and my heart despised reproof? I have not obeyed the voice of my teachers, nor inclined my ear to them that instructed me. I was almost in all evil in the midst of the congregation and assembly."*

Grieve the Loss of Your Minister

And finally, when God takes up your ministers by death from your heads, and you are no more to see their grave faces, nor ever again to hear their gracious words and pleasant voice, mourn humbly before God and cry after them, *"My father, my father, the chariots of Israel and the horsemen thereof,"*

Honor Faithful Christians

Along with your ministers, you may see in the Church of God a great many shining, gracious saints, excellent Christians, some elder, and some younger, whom you ought piously to observe, love, honor and imitate.

You should admire and venerate them for the grace of Christ in them. This will be your piety before God and His people, if His saints be the excellent ones in your eyes and if you honor them that fear the Lord. Let children often remember the unfeigned faith, the bright devotion, the shining meekness, the strict and holy life, of their pious mothers and grandmothers, who are to them as Eunice and Lois were to Timothy. Desire to be like them in the church of Christ, and show that their spirit is in that also. Emulate their goodness, whose names are in the Book of Life. Let parents and tutors instill into young persons this reverence of holy ministers and of godly people.

Honor State Authorities

I come now in the last place to teach young persons how piety should be operating in them toward their superiors in the state or commonwealth: 1. Toward their king, their governor, and magistrates, their civil fathers. 2. Toward persons of eminence for wisdom, learning, ad usefulness. 3. Toward aged persons. 4. Toward the rich and the poor. 5. To their equals and companions.

Children and young people should be piously affected and should behave piously toward their civil fathers, their rulers in the state. Your highest honor and fear is due to these. *"Fear God"* and *"honor the king"* go together. You must render to all their dues, fear to whom fear, and honor to whom honor.

Your king is the Lord's anointed, and is to his people as the breath of their nostrils. You read of old that kings were called Abimelech, the king my father. Think of your king as such. Your governor is sent by him and represents his royal person to you. Your magistrates are the fathers of the country, by birth and education mostly, have all their interest in it, and are its own by choice. They are God's ministers to us for God.

Piety teaches you the greatest inward and outward reverence before them and toward them. Your parents owe submission and obedience to them, and much more you. Job was a grave, wise, and righteous ruler, and he tells us that when he went out to the gate through the city (the gate was the place of judicature), the young men saw him and hid themselves and the aged arose and stood up. Piety teaches youth modesty, and the elders to show respect in the presence of their governor. You must submit yourselves to every ordinance of man for the Lord's sake. Gratitude demands this of you, for from your infancy you have been protected and defended, you and your parents also, by the good government which God has set over you. It was because of them, under God's favor, that you were not torn by enemies, robbers, or murderers; torn from your mothers' breasts in the year when you were born, or that you now enjoy one safe and quiet night.

Pray for Civil Rulers

Children, pray for your rulers and give thanks to God for them. Pray for your excellent governor, who heartily seeks your peace. Pray for all that are in authority, *"that we may lead a quiet and peaceable life in all godliness and reverence. For this is good and acceptable in the sight of God our Savior"* (1 Tim. 2:2-3). Never learn to despise government. *"Those who walk according to the flesh in the lust of uncleanness ... despise authority. They are presumptuous, self-willed. They are not afraid to speak evil of dignitaries"* (2 Pet. 2:10). Because God has dignified and put honor on your rulers, you ought to fear to do them the least dishonor.

It may be that they find grace to be faithful to God, as Moses was, and like Samuel, can affirm their integrity. Must it not be sinful then and dangerous to murmur against them? *"Why then were you not afraid To speak against My servant Moses"* (Num. 12:8)? *"You shall not revile God, nor curse a ruler of your people"* (Ex. 22:28). He that represents him as vile and exercrable, where he deserves it not, he curses him. You read how miserably Dathan and Abiram perished, the earth opened its mouth and swallowed them up, and they went down alive shrieking into the pit. One piteous and lamentable thing in the sin and ruin of these men was that their wives, their sons, and their little children came out in defiance to God and His servant Moses, and stood in the door of their tents with them, and went down with them. Oh! The children should have fled from their rash parents that dreadful day and they would have lived and been blessed by God! Let parents, tutors, and ministers instill into young people the principles of loyalty, honor, and subjection to government.

Honor Toward Prominent People

There are in the commonwealth persons of eminence for wisdom, learning, virtue, and various excellent endowments, who may not be in any place of power. It is wisdom for young people to observe, love, and honor the gifts of God in them, and the image of God upon them. Learn from them, desire to be such yourselves in your generation, and beg of God to make you such.

Honor to the Aged

Young people owe a piety unto the aged. Let the hoary head, found in the ways of righteousness, be a crown of glory in your youthful eyes. It is some faint image of Moses with his shining hair after He had been long on the mount. Christ does not disdain to represent His own eternity by this dim visage of age with us, *"His head and hair were white like wool, as white as snow, and His eyes like a flame of fire"* (Rev. 1:14). No wonder then that He has made it His law to you, young person, *"You shall rise before the gray headed and honor the presence of an old man, and fear your God: I am the Lord"* (Lev. 19:32).

Bearing With Infirmities

This law of our God is doubtless given with such solemnity, because young people are apt to despise or neglect the aged for their infirmities. But piety and discretion will teach you to bear with and cover their infirmities, to entreat them as father, to speak of them and to them with decency, to be modest and silent often before them, to consult and advise with them, for with the aged is experience and wisdom; to believe them, for they know; and hasten to them for they love you and seek your good.

To oblige, serve, and help them that their soul may bless you, to desire their prayers and prize their blessing, to repent of having disobliged and offended them and ask their forgiveness, to mind their heavenly walk and godly end. Desire their life and mourn at their death, for the world loses the benefit of their example, faith and prayers. Let the aged be in behavior as becomes holiness before young people, to command their reverence.

Honor Toward Rich and Poor

4. Young people should behave piously toward the rich and the poor. Learn not to value men merely for their rich estate, their gold ring and goodly apparel, which are apt to take away the eyes and hearts of simple youth. No, children! Let your adorning be the hidden man of the heart, in that which is not corruptible, an ornament of a wise and gracious spirit, which is in the sight of God, of great price. Honor that wherever you see it, whether it be in a poor man or a rich one. Yet, where God gives riches to a man, and advances him hereby in outward rank above some of his neighbors, He calls you to pay unto him a particular outward respect, which at last you give the providence of God.

But be sure that you never despise the poor because he is poor. I would particularly direct that counsel and charge to the children of the rich. Be humble and respectful to the poor. It will please God and honor you among the people of God.

The Poor Are Not Inferior

Think not, young person, that your father's poor neighbor is your inferior, by no means. Especially do not act proudly against him if he is ancient. If he is pious treat him as if he were great and rich; seek his prayers and hear his words.

Learn from your parents (we hope they will teach you), to be full of tender pity and goodness to the poor while you are young. Love to see your parents give to them, and to be the secret carriers of their charity. But let me warn you, children, of a very cruel and barbarous piece of rudeness to the poor and miserable, which we sometimes have seen with grief in our streets. I mean you insulting and abusing a poor creature in rage, in drink, or crazed. It is an unchristian and evil thing in you to do so. Piety will teach you more humanity. Fear God my child, and thank Him that you are not that miserable, nor born of him. Say, did not He that made me in the womb make him? And did not one God fashion us in the womb?

Honor Toward Companions

5. And lastly, young people have their equals, their acquaintance and companions and these must show piety in their conversation together. Be sober, grave, chaste, religious, and as cheerful as you will. Keep no evil company. Walk with the wise and be wiser and make them wiser. Foolish and wicked companions destroy one another. Serve one another's souls. Walk together towards heaven.

Watch and Pray

Watch over and admonish one another. Speak often to each other of God and Christ and holiness, of life and death and hell, of heaven and eternal glories. Pray one for another apart. Combine and meet to pray together, as some of you do. Show to oine another that you fear God. Encourage and assist one another in every thing that is holy and good and so edify yourselves together. Edify one another in love. Honor in one another whatsoever things are honest, pure, lovely, and of good report. If there be any virtue, if there be any praise, think of these things and emulate them. Imitate them in each other.

Thus, young people, I have (in the plainest method and most pressing words that I could) laid before you that piety toward men which is incumbent on you as Christian children. Thus you must honor your parents, magistrates, ministers, tutors, and masters. Yea, you shall honor all men.

In doing this, you will greatly honor and please God, bring glory to His name in your early days, and secure to yourselves His favor and blessing, which is more than life.

All this you owe to your Father in heaven. He has required it of you. He is our fathers' God and you must thus exalt Him, in a conspicuous early piety before men which, when they behold, they will give glory to Him.

So live to your parents' joy, your teachers' pride, your pastors' crown, the delight of mankind, and inherit their joint blessing. The eyes that see you will bless you, and in you will Israel bless God before whom your fathers walked, the God which led them into and fed them in this wilderness. The angel which redeemed them and their posterity from all evil unto this day, bless you, our children, the God of Abraham, Isaac, and Jacob whose name is named on you, bless you, as He has promised to them that keep this commandment, and make you to grow into a multitude in the midst of the earth.

4

EARLY PIETY & SOBER MINDEDNESS

Mr. Joseph Sewall, Boston, April 13, 1721

Titus 2:6
Likewise, exhort the young men to be sober-minded.

The apostle Paul, having laid the foundation of a Christian church in the island of Crete, left Titus, the evangelist, there to set in order the things that were wanting and to ordain elders in every city (Titus 1:5). That Titus might better perform the duties of his office, the apostle furnished him with several excellent instructions respecting his doctrine and life. Among others, we have this direction relating to young persons. Young men are to be *"exhorted."* The word means, *"to call, to beseech, and comfort"*. *"Young men"* refers to juniors and younger persons. The word is translated, *"younger"* in Luke 22:26. The words,*"To be sober-minded"* in the original signifies to be sober, temperate, chaste, wise, and discreet. The context is to be of a right and sound mind, to govern their affections, appetites, and passions. Therefore, it is a most suitable exhortation for those in the heat of youth, who are so inclined to give the reins to their unruly lusts and exorbitant passions. In a word, it may refer either to the body or mind, and brings a due regulation of both, according to God's Word.

Sober Mindedness

DOCTRINE
It is the duty of young persons to be sober-minded.

The apostle, under the infallible guidance of the Spirit of God, gives this charge to Titus, to exhort. It is written for the instruction of gospel ministers to the end of the world. Here then is the call of God to young persons, both men, and women, to be sober-minded. *"For the grace of God that brings salvation has appeared to all men, teaching us that, denying ungodliness and worldly lusts, we should live soberly, righteously, and godly in the present age"* (Titus 2:11-12).

You have had the duties of Godliness and righteousness explained. It remains for us to consider the duties you stand obliged to perform, respecting yourselves. Indeed, the duties we are now speaking of come under the general heading of justice or righteousness, and are to be referred to the second table of the law. Thus for example, the Seventh Commandment requires the preservation of our own as well as our neighbors' chastity. For the illustration of the doctrine, I will consider several things implied in being sober-minded.

A Mind Under Right Influence

Young persons must take care that their minds be under the governing influence of right principles.

We have observed that the word signifies to be of a right mind. Consider Mark 5:15: He that had been possessed, is said to be *"sitting and clothed and in his right mind."* Now, if we would have a sound mind in a spiritual sense, we must seek to get our minds enlightened with the saving knowledge of the truths of God's Word, and make use of the excellent rules there laid down for the right government of our lives. The apostle Peter exhorts believers, *"Gird up the loins of your mind, be sober"* (1 Pet. 1:13).

Now this girdle is truth, *"having girded your waist with truth"* (Eph. 6:14). This girdle is not only for ornament, but also for strength to the faculties of the soul, that they may not be loosed in an hour of temptation. Therefore, unless young persons wear this girdle, they will be of dissolute lives and manners. The eyes of understanding are the leading faculty, therefore if that is blind, there must be disorder and confusion in the whole man.

It is said that the Gentiles walk in the vanity of their mind, *"having their understanding darkened, being alienated from the life of God, because of the ignorance that is in them, because of the blindness of their heart"* (Eph. 4:17-18). *"Likewise, when their foolish hearts were darkened"*, *"God also gave them up to uncleanness"* (Rom. 1:24).

Those Devoid of Understanding

It is very observable of young persons, that their ignorance, their want of right judgment, prudence, and discretion are often the causes of great irregularities in their conduct and behavior. The youth who yielded to the enticements of the adulteress is called *"a young man devoid of understanding"* (Prov. 7:7).

If you would then, discharge your duty towards yourselves, you must obey that word. *"Say to wisdom, 'You are my sister,' And call understanding your nearest kin"* (Prov. 7:4).

Seeking Wisdom

You must ask God for that wisdom which is from above and treasure up the Word of God in your hearts for the due regulation of your thoughts, words, and actions. If you would think soberly in the great matters of religion, and act as wise men when you grow up to years of understanding, you must not take up your religion merely as a tradition from your fathers.

You should search the Scriptures and read other good books, that you may understand the ground and foundational principles on which it is built, that you should *"no longer be children, tossed to and fro and carried about with every wind of doctrine, by the trickery of men, in the cunning craftiness of deceitful plotting"* (Eph. 4:14). You should hold fast the form of sound words which you have heard, in faith and love, which is in Christ Jesus.

Learning a Catechism

The catechism you generally learn in your childhood is an excellent body of divinity, and well worth the study of your riper years. It might be a very profitable exercise for our young people to get some good exposition on the catechism, and study it with diligence and earnest prayer to God, to lead them into all truth, comparing the doctrines laid down therein, with the texts of Scripture brought to confirm them. To the law and to the testimony! Unless our young people be well established in the doctrines of the gospel, and under the government of the sacred truths delivered there, there will be the greatest danger of their slighting and then betraying that cause of God for which our forefathers came into this land when it was an howling wilderness.

Be Cautious

Young persons must take heed that they are wary, cautious, and deliberate.

Young persons are full of heat and therefore are prone to be too quick and sudden in their motions; too rash and heady in their resolve. They are apt to make up their minds on things of great consequence before they have weighed them well. Now this precipitancy is often the cause of great blunders in their conduct, and in many instances, they have reason to repent at leisure. Therefore, if young persons would be sober-minded, they must look about them. Be willing to take advice of those who are of riper years and of greater experience, and not abound in their own sense.

Above all, you should look up to God in prayer to guide you by His counsel and commit your ways unto Him, crying to Him, *"My Father, You are the guide of my youth"* (Jer. 3:4). With the well-advised there is wisdom. Such will walk circumspectly, not as fools, but as wise. But if you are rash, inadvertent, and lean on your own understanding, you will exalt folly.

Humility

Young persons must be humble, and take heed they
do not think of themselves more highly then they ought.

This is implied in sober-mindedness. *"For I say, through the grace given to me, to everyone who is among you, not to think of himself more highly than he ought to think, but to think soberly"* (Rom. 12:3). It is the same word that is used in our text. Young people must then be humble. You should earnestly seek after such a frame of spirit as the psalmist had, *"Lord, my heart is not haughty, Nor my eyes lofty. Neither do I concern myself with great matters, Nor with things too profound for me"* (Ps. 131:1).

You must humble yourselves, and become as little children, ordinary, and little in your own eyes, or you cannot enter into the Kingdom of heaven. Pride is a lust of the mind, and is a sin which easily besets young persons. *"The child will be insolent toward the elder, and base toward the honorable"* (Isa. 3:5). They are often ignorant of themselves, novices, and so prone to be lifted up with pride, and in danger of falling into the condemnation of the Devil. If young people have wit and superiority, beauty, riches, fine apparel etc., how apt they are to swell with pride! *"There is a generation—oh, how lofty are their eyes! And their eyelids are lifted up"* (Prov. 30:13). Many proclaim this sin in their looks, gestures, and carriages. Thus the daughters of Zion were haughty, and walked with stretched forth necks. Their pride was also declared in the excess of their apparel, for which reason God threatened to take away the finery of their ornaments (Isa. 3:16-18). Young people are apt to be conceited and to magnify themselves, to desire vain glory, and be ambitious of more honor and respect than they deserve.

Cast Down Pride

Let them therefore be deeply humbled for their pride, and by the grace of God, cast down their proud imaginations, and everything that exalts itself against God. Obey that command, *"Likewise you younger people, submit yourselves to your elders. Yes, all of you be submissive to one another, and be clothed with humility"* (1 Pet. 5:5). This grace becomes you. This garment well fits and suits you, for sin has made you naked to your shame. It is pleasing to God, but the opposite is abominable in his sight. *"Everyone proud in heart is an abomination to the Lord"* (Prov. 16:5). God resists the proud, and gives grace to the humble. Humble yourselves then, that God may exalt you. Beware of pride, lest God be provoked to leave you some sin which will be a blot and stain that will cleave to you, and not be wiped away. O remember that word, *"Pride goes before destruction, And a haughty spirit before a fall"* (Prov, 16:18).

Meek and Quiet Spirit

> *Young persons must see that they are of a meek and quiet spirit.*

Meekness is a grace of the Holy Spirit, whereby we regulate our anger, according to the rules of God's Word. Now the contrary sin, rash and immoderate anger often prevails in young people, who have a natural fervor of spirit in conjunction with a vicious disposition to this sin. How soon do we observe wrathful passions working in our children! Now, this is a great sin and leads to other sins. Persons overcome by passion often curse, swear and call wicked names, sins that are highly provoking to God. Our young people should carefully avoid, and shun this temptation. To be angry with our brother without a cause or in an undue measure is a breach of the Sixth Commandment, and it leads to more heinous violations of it. How often do men smite their neighbor with the fit of wickedness when in the heat of passion! Yea, this sin has produced bloody effects and has even led to murder.

The Shechemites

We have the dreadful example in the slaughter of the Shechemite by Simeon and Levi, of which Jacob speaks, *"Let not my soul enter their council; Let not my honor be united to their assembly; For in their anger they slew a man, And in their self-will they hamstrung an ox. Cursed be their anger, for it is fierce; And their wrath, for it is cruel"* (Gen. 49:6-7)!

Let us all, particularly our young people, obey that command: *"Put on tender mercies, kindness, humility, meekness, longsuffering; bearing with one another"* (Col, 3:12-13).

Gentleness

O young persons! Be gentle, and easily entreated, not wrathful and revengeful. Avoid this great sin, and all the occasions of it, as grievous words, which stir up anger (Prov. 15:1). It is true, we may be angry, but sin not (Eph. 4:26). But then, when we are angry without cause or in undue measure, when we retain it, when we let the sun go down on our wrath, and when we allow our anger to degenerate into malice and hatred, we break God's law and are found transgressors. We do that which is sinful and displeasing in His sight, as well as hurtful and dishonorable to ourselves. *"Whoever is angry with his brother without a cause shall be in danger of the judgment"* (Matt. 5:22). Individuals who act in this manner do expose themselves to the righteous judgment of God and also to manifold mischiefs from men. *"Whoever has no rule over his own spirit is like a city broken down, without walls"* (Prov. 25:28). How naked and exposed are such!

Let our young people then be deeply humbled for their rash anger and passion. If you have, at any time, been filled with rage at your parents or masters for giving you needful correction, fly to the blood of Jesus Christ for pardon and ask of God His Spirit, for the fruit of the Spirit, which includes gentleness and meekness (Gal. 5:22-23). O take heed that you do not give up yourselves to rash anger and passion, which is a short madness! Watch over your hearts and pray to God to keep them and to enable you to govern your passion.

Meekness is an Ornament

A meek and quiet spirit is an excellent spirit indeed: *"The incorruptible beauty of a gentle and quiet spirit ... is very precious in the sight of God"* (1 Pet. 3:4). O seek this ornament and never forget to wear it! Such a spirit is pleasing to God, lovely in the eyes of men, and of great benefit to societies. Their well-being very much depends upon this, that the various members put off wrath, anger, and malice - for the tranquility and good order of families. Much depends on young men and women to take care to govern their passion. Where an angry spirit prevails, there will be strife and then confusion and every evil work. One character in the description of the perilous times of the last days is that men will be *"brutal"* (2 Tim. 3:3). O, fly from this sin then, and follow after meekness.

Moderation

Young persons must be moderate in their desires and pursuits of sensual pleasures.

Beza interprets the words, *"Exhort young men that they be moderate and without question,"* as a moderation of our desires of carnal pleasures. One thing is intended in this exhortation, for this is what persons in the vigor and heat of youth are exceeding prone to and have been often cast down by. At this age, you have the highest liking and relish for the most exquisite sense of carnal pleasures. This is a bait which Satan frequently, and alas, how successfully, uses to catch young people in an evil net. That may often be given as the character of young people, *"lovers of pleasure rather than lovers of God"* (2 Tim. 3:4). They are for play and pastime. This and that diversion consume their precious time. They are ready to say with the rich fool, *"Soul, take thine ease, eat drink and be merry,"* and to promise themselves that tomorrow will be as this day and more abundant. They put far away the evil day and then loose their sensual inclinations. Accordingly, the royal preacher speaks to young persons,

"Rejoice, O young man, in your youth, And let your heart cheer you in the days of your youth; Walk in the ways of your heart, And in the sight of your eyes; But know that for all these God will bring you into judgment" (Eccl. 11:9).

By this ironical concession, the wise man implies that the hearts of people are set on their pleasures, but then he checks them by calling upon them to remember the day of judgment when God will reckon with them, and give them sorrow and torment according to their living in sinful pleasures. O be exhorted therefore, to moderate and mortify your love of pleasures which has slain their ten thousands! Flee those youthful lusts which war against the soul. Abstain wholly from such pleasures that are forbidden, and take care to use those delights which are in themselves lawful, to not abuse them.

Time

O do not waste your precious time, which is so short and uncertain, in sports and recreations. Use your time in such a manner that you may be prepared for serious employments and weighty business. These pleasures immoderately indulge, blind the mind, stupefy the conscience, debauch the affections, and make you carnal, sensual, and brutish. They choke the good seed of the word.

Though they are but for a season, if you live in them, they will drown your souls in eternal perdition and bring you to that place where is weeping and gnashing of teeth forever. Look to God then, for His grace, and by the Spirit mortify these deeds of the flesh. Surely it is better to cut off a right hand or pluck out a right eye than to be cast into that fire which cannot be quenched. The time would fail me to mention all the delights and pleasures whereby young persons are ensnared and ruined.

Temperate

Young persons must be temperate.

We are commanded to add to knowledge *"self control"* (2 Pet. 1:6). I use the word here in a restrained sense, for a due regulation of the appetite respecting meat and drink. Now this is a considerable branch of sobriety and a duty incumbent on all, particularly on young people. Be persuaded then, to hearken to the counsel given you. *"Hear, my son, and be wise; And guide your heart in the way. Do not mix with winebibbers, Or with gluttonous eaters of meat; For the drunkard and the glutton will to poverty"* (Prov. 23:19-21).

Stubborness Judged

There was a law of old which threatened death to such wicked young men who persisted in these sins, notwithstanding the admonitions of these parents.

"If a man has a stubborn and rebellious son who will not obey the voice of his father or the voice of his mother, and who, when they have chastened him, will not heed them, then his father and his mother shall take hold of him and bring him out to the elders of his city, to the gate of his city. And they shall say to the elders of his city, 'This son of ours is stubborn and rebellious; he will not obey our voice; he is a glutton and a drunkard.' Then all the men of his city shall stone him to death with stones" (Deut. 21:18-21).

You see here that the incorrigible youth who would not be reclaimed from such sins, was to be put to death. Know that these sins of gluttony and drunkenness are no less provoking to God under the gospel dispensation, than they were under the law. Such works of darkness are more heinous in the sight of God when committed under the light of the glorious gospel. Agreeably, we have those words, *"Let us walk properly, as in the day, not in revelry and drunkenness"* (Rom. 13:13). Take heed then, lest at any time your hearts be overcharged with forfeiting and drunkenness. Manifold are the mischievous consequences; and bitter fruits of this sin. *"Wine, and new wine enslave the heart"* (Hosea 4:11). This sin strangely besets and infatuates men, and makes them vile. Such excesses cloud and enfeeble the mind, and take off the heart from all that is good. Those who drink to excess will forget the law, and will be in the utmost hazard of falling into many foolish and hurtful lusts. [1]

Drunkeness

"Wine is a mocker, Strong drink is a brawler" (Prov. 20:1). If you enflame yourselves with it, you may be left to take God's dreadful name in vain, and to scoff at all that is serious. Who has woe? Who has sorrow? Who has contentions? Who has redness of eyes? They that tarry long at the wine, that go to seek mixed wine. Again, this sin mars the beauty and sprightliness of youth. It wastes it, and renders it a fading flower. But what is inconceivably more hurtful, sin wounds the precious soul and provokes God to withdraw even the common restraints of His grace.

This sin quenches the motions of God's Holy Spirit. *"Do not be drunk with wine, in which is dissipation; but be filled with the Spirit"* (Eph. 5:18). If sin be persisted in, it will destroy body and soul in hell. Drunkards are numbered among them that shall not inherit the kingdom of God (1 Cor. 6:10). Such must be washed, sanctified, and justified in the name of the Lord Jesus, and by the Spirit of our God, or be cast out of God's presence forever. Let us all then, and particularly our young people, be exhorted to flee from these sins. When you eat and drink, let it be for strength and not for drunkenness. Do not frequent taverns and indulge yourselves in night-revels.

It is a shame and scandal for young men, or any others, to be at public houses or inflaming themselves with strong drink, when they should be in their closets, praying to that God who seeth in secret, or attending family-duties, or at rest in their beds. Take heed then, have no fellowship with such unfruitful works of darkness, but rather reprove them. This sin may seem pleasant now, but know that *"At the last it bites like a serpent, And stings like a viper. Your eyes will see strange things, And your heart will utter perverse things. Yes, you will be like one who lies down in the midst of the sea, Or like one who lies at the top of the mast"* (Prov. 23:32-34).

---

1. Our Excellent *George Herbert* well expresses this,
He that is drunken, may his Mother kill,
Big with his sister; He hath lost the reigns,
Is out-lawed by himself: All kind of ill,
Did with his liquor slide into his veins. ["The Church Porch, stanza 6]

Purity

Young people must be chaste.

This is an eminent branch of sobriety and it is a great duty commanded in God's law. The Seventh Commandment is, *"You shall not commit adultery"* (Ex. 20:14). It requires chastity in body, mind, in thoughts, words, and actions, and forbids all filthiness and uncleanness. We now especially consider it as it concerns young people and such as are in a single state. It must be said to young people as well as others, *"This is the will of God, your sanctification: that you should abstain from sexual immorality; that each of you should know how to possess his own vessel in sanctification and honor"* (1 Thess. 4:3-4).

Avoid Impurity

Take heed to yourselves, to avoid all impurity, and all means and provocations thereunto. You must, by the grace of God, keep yourselves from all uncleanness in heart, speech, and behavior. If you would be sober-minded, you must get the inward lusting of the heart subdued and mortified.

The Seventh Commandment

We are told that these are a breach of the Seventh Commandment (Matt. 5:28). And thus, our Savior also assures us that *"out of the heart proceed evil thoughts, murders, adulteries, fornications, thefts, false witness, blasphemies. These are the things which defile a man"* (Matt. 15:19-20).

Therefore, there must be great care taken to abstain from lustful thoughts and impure imaginations. We must take heed that we do not entertain and defile our minds with filthy speculations and burn with unclean desires.

Mortify Lust

On the contrary, we must mortify evil sexual desires, lest we be led aside by our own lust and enticed. You must also take care that you do not yield any of the parts of your bodies as instruments to uncleanness. The countenance and outward gestures are the index of the mind, and therefore, you must take care that these be grave and modest, that you be not light and wanton in your looks and gestures.

The Eyes

We read of a wicked person that *"winks"* with his eyes, *"shuffles"* his feet, and *"points with his fingers"* (Prov. 6:13). The eye is a window through which much sin is let into the soul and therefore, if you would preserve your chastity, you must make a covenant with your eyes, as Job did (Job 31:1). Take heed that you are not as they who have eyes full of adultery.

Your Speech

Again, you must look to God to keep the door of your lips and refrain from that evil communication which corrupts good manners. *"Let no corrupt word proceed out of your mouth"* (Eph. 4:29). *"Let your speech always be with grace, seasoned with salt"* (Col. 4:6). Let your tongues be employed in the singing the praises of God, and not in singing filthy songs. O do not turn your glory into shame, by employing the power of speech to such vile purposes!

Corrupt Conversations

And then take heed that you do not listen to the corrupt communications of others. Again, take heed, and beware of all wanton dalliances and impure touches. To be sure then, you must take heed and beware of all gross acts of filthiness, whether alone, or with others.

By this, we may sufficiently understand how wicked and abominable a practice this is amongst Christians and in the light of the gospel. It lays greater and stricter obligations upon us to purity and severely forbids all filthiness of flesh and spirit. Young persons must keep themselves pure and not allow themselves to be involved in any acts of filthiness with others. They must take heed to themselves that they do not entice others to sin.

Remember Joseph

If they are enticed, they must answer as Joseph replied to the impure solicitations of his mistress, *"How then can I do this great wickedness, and sin against God"* (Gen. 39:9)? You must avoid the company of such, as you would persons that have some deadly infectious distemper, and not consent to be with them or to give them an opportunity to repeat their solicitations (Prov. 5:3-12).

Fornication

This sin committed between single persons is a great breach of God's law, and not to be accounted a light matter. Even for betrothed people to come together before a marriage be consummated is not to be accounted a small sin. No! It is a dishonor to God, a scandal to religion, and to be carefully avoided by all.

Adultery

It is a more heinous transgression of the Seventh Commandment for people to commit this sin where one or both are in a married state, as this is a horrid violation of the marriage covenant, which God calls His covenant, and accordingly was of old punished with death. *"The man who commits adultery with another man's wife, he who commits adultery with his neighbor's wife, the adulterer and the adulteress, shall surely be put to death"* (Lev. 20:10).

Incest

It is a great aggravation of this sin for close kinship to commit this sin together. Of this great sin of incest we may read Leviticus 18:6-18. Marriage cannot make this lawful, for all marriages contrary to the law of God are null and void. God does not join such persons together. Again, it is a high aggravation of this sin when violence is included in the commission of it, as Ammon forced his sister, Tamar (2 Sam. 13:14). A horrid crime! There are other violations of the Seventh Commandment which it might well fill one with horror, to think that any should be guilty of. But I pass them over in silence. O that such abominations may never be committed in our land!

Flee Uncleaness

Let us all, and particularly our young people, be exhorted to flee this great sin of uncleanness in all the degrees, kinds, and branches of it. This is a youthful lust, a sin which, as in the heat and strength of youth, are peculiarly disposed to and in danger of.

"For at the window of my house I looked through my lattice, And saw among the simple, I perceived among the youths, A young man devoid of understanding, Passing along the street near her corner; And he took the path to her house In the twilight, in the evening, In the black and dark night. And there a woman met him, With the attire of a harlot, and a crafty heart" (Prov. 7:6-10).

"With her enticing speech she caused him to yield, With her flattering lips she seduced him. Immediately he went after her, as an ox goes to the slaughter, Or as a fool to the correction of the stocks, Till an arrow struck his liver. As a bird hastens to the snare, He did not know it would cost his life. Now therefore, listen to me, my children; Pay attention to the words of my mouth: Do not let your heart turn aside to her ways, Do not stray into her paths; For she has cast down many wounded, And all who were slain by her were strong men" (Prov. 7:21-26).

The Damage Done

That you may be excited to flee this sin, consider the heinous nature, and dreadful consequences of it: it imprints a special mark of dishonor and infamy on the body. *"He who commits sexual immorality sins against his own body"* (1 Cor. 6:18). It consumes the body (Prov. 5:11). Whoredom and wine take away the heart. It is a wound to our good name. *"Wounds and dishonor he will get, and his reproach will not be wiped away"* (Prov. 6:33). It has both a natural and moral tendency to shorten life. *"His bones are full of his youthful vigor, but it will lie down with him in the dust"* (Job 20:11). *"They die in youth, and their life ends among the perverted persons"* (Job 36:14).

In a word, it destroys the precious soul, and exposes to dreadful judgments in this world, and that which is to come, *"Fornicators and adulterers God will judge"* (Heb. 13:4). Such may hide their sins from men, but they cannot escape the righteous judgment of God, nor the vengeance of eternal fire, unless they repent and fly to Christ.

Eternal Punishment

This sin persisted in will shut you out of heaven and provoke God to cast you down where the worm never dieth. *"Do not be deceived. Neither fornicators, nor idolaters, nor adulterers, nor homosexuals, nor sodomites, nor thieves, nor covetous, nor drunkards, nor revilers, nor extortioners will inherit the kingdom of God"* (1 Cor. 6:9-10). The wise man speaks of those who are given up to this sin as abhorred of the Lord. *"The mouth of an immoral woman is a deep pit; He who is abhorred by the Lord will fall there"* (Prov. 22:14).

Repent

If we have then been guilty of this sin, in any degree or kind, we should be deeply humbled in the sight of God, and go to the fountain which is set open for sin and uncleanness to the blood of Christ which cleanses from all sin. We should ask the Holy Spirit to wash us from our filthiness, and cry to God to create a clean heart within us. A clean heart will preserve us from this sin.

Immodesty

We should abhor the company of unchaste and wanton persons. We should also observe a decorum in our garb and dress, as well as look and gesture. *"In like manner also, that the women adorn themselves in modest apparel, with propriety and moderation"* (1 Tim. 2:9).

Again, we must avoid the sin of idleness which leads to this, and many other sins. One of the sins of Sodom was the abundance of idleness. We must be diligent in some lawful calling. When it is needful, we must use that remedy which God has provided: *"Nevertheless, because of sexual immorality, let each man have his own wife, and let each woman have her own husband"* (1 Cor. 7:2). And then take care that we preserve conjugal fidelity and purity.

Frugality

Young persons must be frugal and thrifty.

You must avoid prodigality and profuseness and take heed that you be not as the prodigal son, who wasted his substance with riotous living (Luke 15:13). If your parents have left you an estate or you have, in other ways, gotten one, you must consider this is a talent which God has lent you and one which He requires you to employ in His service and for His glory. Take heed therefore, that you do not waste it to gratify your ambition or sensuality. Do not attempt to make a greater show than your estate will bear. Do not presume that what God has given you depends upon your gifts.

Gambling

Particularly, beware of the sin of gambling, which is a breach of the Eighth Commandment. The money which is lost by gambling is vilely cast away and that which is gotten by it is dishonestly gotten and must be restored, or it may be a moth to your whole estate. In a word, see to it that you do not waste your estates, or what may be given you by your parents, in unlawful recreations and pleasures, or by the immoderate use of such as are in themselves innocent and lawful.

Presuming on God's Mercy

I may say that young persons must take heed and beware of carnal confidence and presumption. Do not presume God's mercy while you persist in sin. Do not be so presumptuous as to promise yourselves a more convenient season for working out your salvation, when God says, *"Today, if you will hear His voice, Do not harden your hearts"* (Heb. 3:7-8). Do not imagine that God will always strive with you, or that it is in your power to repent. Such vain and impious imaginations are repugnant to sober-mindedness, and prove pernicious to many young people, who hope by presumption, and so perish.

APPLICATION

Application I. *If this is the duty of young men, then such as are of riper years should be sober-minded.*

Middle-aged and elder persons should take care that their moderation and due regulation of their appetites be conspicuous. It is your duty to be examples of prudence, meekness, temperance, etc. Thus, you should teach young persons sobriety by your well-ordered conversation.

Application II. *Let us look back on the sins and follies of our youth and be deeply humbled.*

The best of us have abundant reason to lament the sinful follies and miscarriages of our youth; for childhood and youth are vanity (Eccl. 11:10). Let us reflect upon them with deep abasement, mourn after a godly sort upon the account of them, and fly to the grace and mercy of God in Jesus Christ for pardon and cleansing. Who can understand his errors? Lord cleanse us from secret faults. Remember not the sins of our youth, nor our transgressions, according to Your mercy. remember us, for Your goodness sake, O Lord. If the Lord should mark iniquities, the iniquities of our youth, we will not be able to stand.

Let us then have our entire dependence on Jesus Christ for righteousness. Unless your sins are covered they are all remembered by God against you, as if committed but yesterday. We need, therefore, to be earnest with God to blot out our transgressions according to the multitude of His tender mercies. If we are converted, we should strengthen our younger brethren and children. The memory of the temptations and sins of our youth should excite our tender compassion toward our young people, and quicken us to do our utmost to preserve them, or recover them, if fallen into sin.

Application III. *Let our young people be exhorted to be sober-minded.*

I beseech you, suffer the word of exhortation which is given to you now in the name of the Lord. Do your duty towards yourselves in the exercise of a regular self-love. Govern your appetites and passions according to the rules of God's Word. To this end, O young person! Know yourself, learn from God's Word how you were formed in your first parents, and how vile and wretched you are by the fall. Reverence yourself; consider the excellent powers and faculties with which God has endowed you. God, your Maker, teaches you *"more than the beasts of the earth,"* and makes you *"wiser than the birds of heaven"* (Job 35:11).

Do Not Be Stubborn

Do not be as the horse or as the mule, which have no understanding. You have a precious immortal soul within you, capable of knowing, glorifying, and enjoying God forever. O do not make it a slave to your lusts and vile affections. Do not mar and destroy God's workmanship. The loss is your own if you do, and who can declare how great a loss this is to lose your soul forever? Cry to God to renew you in the spirit of your minds, that being born of the Spirit, you may be enabled to discharge these duties from a gracious principle, and with a sincere aim at God's glory.

Learn from Christ

Put on Christ and make no provision for the flesh to fulfill it in the lusts thereof. Learn from Him who was meek and lowly, harmless and undefiled. Walk in the Spirit, and you will not fulfill the lusts of the flesh.
And now, let us cry to God to pour out His Spirit upon us and upon our children, that by the grace of God, which has appeared to us, we may be taught to live soberly, righteously, and godly in this present world.

OBLIGATIONS *of* EARLY PIETY

Mr. Prince, Boston, April 27, 1721

Proverbs 23:26
My son, give me your heart.

This book is called the Proverbs, because it is a divine collection of the proverbs, i.e. the wise and pithy sentences of Solomon, the son of David, king of Israel. The great design in general is to bring the sons of men to know wisdom and instruction, to perceive the words of understanding, and to receive the instruction of wisdom, justice and judgment and equity. In particular, Proverbs are to give wisdom to the simple, and to the young man, knowledge and discretion. Thus, He tells us himself in the four first verses.

As King Solomon excelled all the earth in wisdom, so he was renowned also for his excellent sayings. It is said he spoke three thousand proverbs. *"And men of all nations, from all the kings of the earth who had heard of his wisdom, came to hear the wisdom of Solomon"* (1 Kings 4:32-34).

Prophesy Fulfilled

In these excellent proverbs, he dispensed his wisdom. Like Moses, his doctrine dropped as the rain all about him, his speech distilled as the dew, as the small rain upon the tender herb, and as the showers upon the grass (Deut. 32:2).

In this respect, that prophecy of his father David was accomplished in him. *"He shall come down like rain upon the grass before mowing, Like showers that water the earth"* (Ps. 72:6). And on this account it seems to be that when the Queen of Sheba had seen his wisdom, the seating of his servants, and the attendance of his ministers; she cried out to the king in admiration,

"It was a true report which I heard in my own land about your words and your wisdom. However I did not believe their words until I came and saw with my own eyes; and indeed the half of the greatness of your wisdom was not told me. You exceed

the fame of which I heard. Happy are your men and happy are these your servants, who stand continually before you and hear your wisdom" (2 Chron. 9:5-7).

Happy were they that continually stood before him and heard these wise and excellent proverbs proceed from his mouth! Happy are we that have them copied out and set before us, that we may continually read and study them, but most happy those that carefully observe and follow them. By receiving these instructions of wisdom, we will become wise like him that governs them. They will give even more wisdom to those that are simple, and to the young man knowledge and discretion.

Instruction for Youth

And indeed in the midst of all his speeches, we may plainly observe that this most wise and foreseeing king had a singular view to the rising generation. He clearly saw of what importance it was to instruct the youth in the principles of wisdom, and that these were the likeliest and the fittest to learn them.

Those grown up in years had spent their time; their season of service would soon be over, and they were so thoroughly fixed and riveted in their several ways and principles, that they were not so like to learn or receive instruction. The good had received it and were wise already and had less need to be taught than others. He did not need to take many pains with these, for they would hear and increase in learning, and of their own accord aspire to higher degrees of wisdom and knowledge.

The wicked had received such ill and deep impressions from their long continuance in their sinful courses, that there was little hope of their hearkening to him.

"The wicked are estranged from the womb; They go astray as soon as they are born, speaking lies. Their poison is like the poison of a serpent; They are like the deaf cobra that stops its ear, Which will not heed the voice of charmers, Charming ever so skillfully" (Ps. 58:3-5).

The tender youth were the most fit and apt to learn, and the easiest and likeliest to receive instruction. They were the springing supports of the rising age, and if these could be imbued with wisdom, how wise and happy would be the next generation? King Solomon sees it, and he therefore continually fixes his eye upon them. He shows a singular regard to them in his wise speeches and immortal writings.

Books for Youth

It seems indeed as if the books of the Proverbs and Ecclesiastes were written chiefly for the instruction of youth. For the book of the Proverbs begins thus: *"My son, hear the instruction of your father"* (Prov.1:8). Throughout the whole book, he continually returns to this peculiar expression, *"My son, my son,"* and a learned man observes that he repeats this address twenty-three times to show that the main end of his writing was the instruction of young ones.

Similarly, the book of the Ecclesiastes ends with such words as these: *"And further, my son, be admonished by these. Of making many books there is no end, and much study is wearisome to the flesh. Let us hear the conclusion of the whole matter: Fear God and keep His commandments, For this is man's all"* (Eccl.12:12-13).

This great and renowned king condescends to be a preacher to children. He speaks to every child about him when he says, *"my son,"* and he calls upon them by this endearing term in our text, to express his tender affection, and engage them toward him.

But we must here remember that Solomon was a divinely inspired preacher, and he does not speak so much in his own name as in the name of God that employed and moved him. It is in the name of God, and to God Himself that he requests the youth to give his heart. The wise man does not speak these words on his own behalf, but on the behalf of God, whose messenger he was.

Indeed, if we judge aright, they are the words of God Himself by this inspired preacher. Like as the apostle tells us, he and other ministers were ambassadors employed by Christ and by them even God and Christ entreated men to be *"reconciled to God"* (2 Cor. 5:20). It is God, our heavenly Father, who most earnestly desires this gift from youth and children to be presented to Him, and to whom it is most especially and principally due.

In the name of God, I require you therefore now to yield obedience to this great and important doctrine:

DOCTRINE
Youth and children must give up their hearts to God in their early days.

As this great and royal preacher did, so I now apply myself to the youth and children round about me. I, though most unworthy, speak by the same authority. I am the minister of God unto you. I come with the same design. I deliver you the same message. It is the word and voice of God Himself, and in His name I plainly tell you. God tells you by me, that you must now give up your hearts to God in your youthful age.

For illustration I will endeavor to communicate these two things: first, to show you what it is to give up your hearts to God, and secondly, to describe the great and solemn obligations that you are to obey.

The first of these I will be very brief upon, because the nature of early piety, as it relates to God, our neighbor, and ourselves, has already been explained and set before you. The latter I will more largely address, it being my peculiar province to set before the children of our people, the great and solemn obligations they are under to be religious in their youthful age.

First, What it is to give up your hearts to God?

Now, to give up your hearts to God is to give up yourselves to God entirely and forever through Christ, and with all your hearts.

It is to give up yourselves and all you have entirely to Him in your early days. You must give up your bodies and all its parts and members and especially the tongue to God. You must give up all your senses to Him: your strength and vigor, and your health and beauty. You must likewise give up your spirit, temper, and all your various appetites and passions to Him. And in addition, you must also give up your most precious souls, with all their faculties, abilities and powers to God: your imagination, understanding, reason, judgment, conscience, affections, will, and memory. Finally, you must give up all your knowledge, cleverness and ingenuity, and all the treasures and endowments of your minds. You must give them all to God without the least reserve.

All That You Are

For what ends and purposes must you give them to Him? I answer, you must give them all to God, to be sanctified, possessed, and governed by Him. You must give them up to be His own inheritance and property. You must give them up, to live, move, and act for God and to be improved entirely for His interest and service. You must give up yourselves to seek and know Him, and to adore and serve Him. You must entirely give up yourselves to God, to be disposed of as He sees good, to study to know His mind and will, and to do and suffer whatever He requires of you. You must give up yourselves, *"denying ungodliness and worldly lusts, [that] we should live soberly, righteously, and godly in the present age"* (Titus 2:12). You must give up yourselves in eating, drinking, or whatever else you do, that you may do it *"to the glory of God"* (1 Cor. 10:31). And finally, you must give up yourselves to God, to have communion with Him and enjoy Him, to be filled with all His fullness, and to be made completely like Him.

All That You Have

In giving up yourselves to God, you must also give up all you have. You must give up your very lives and all your powers of speaking, thought, and action. You must devote your studies, learning, interest, honor, and reputation to God. Your recreations, pleasures, affairs and time, and, to be sure, whatever you esteem and value, you must give up to God. In short, you must give Him all you own, can suffer, do, or enjoy. You must keep nothing from Him. You entirely resign and devote them to Him, and you must give them up, to be subordinated and improved for His own glory, and to be disposed of according to His sovereign pleasure.

Eternal Adoration

You must therefore give up yourselves to God forever. God will have you for His own forever, or not at all. He would have you be in an eternal subjection to Him. He would have you be the eternal active instruments of His glory and honor. God would have you yield eternal adoration to Him. He would have you to be the eternal objects of His delight and love, and He would have you to be forever happy in the service and enjoyment of Him.

You must therefore give up yourselves and all you have to God, forever. You must make such an absolute devotion of yourselves to God; as never to have the least pretence or right, to free yourselves again. You must give up yourselves entirely to God in an everlasting covenant, never to be broken. And this, O children, you must do in your early days.

All to Christ

You must give up yourselves to God in Christ. Children! Apart from Christ, God will not accept you. God has indeed an unalienable right and propriety in you. You must be His own forever, and He will eternally use you for His glory. But apart from Christ, He will surely make you the miserable instruments of the dreadful glory of His power and justice, and not the happy instruments of the glory of His grace and mercy. You are both by life and nature most abominable and guilty sinners, and apart from Christ, God utterly abhors you and is angry with you. He cannot accept, He cannot forgive, and He cannot be reconciled to you. But in Christ, His Son and our Mediator, God is reconcilable to such sinful children, and He is ready to forgive you and receive you (2 Cor. 5:18-19).

You must therefore give yourselves to God in Christ or He will cast you off. You must, in the first place, go to Christ the Son of God and your Mediator. You must present and give yourselves to Christ, that He may give you unto God. You must plead with Christ to accept and take you for His own and you must not doubt but that He will receive you, since He was so displeased with those that hindered children from coming to Him, and said *"Let the little children come to Me, and do not forbid them; for of such is the kingdom of God"* (Mark 10:12-16).

Therefore, children, you must not doubt that Christ will accept and bless you upon your coming and giving up yourselves unto Him. And then, in Christ, you may with a holy confidence give up yourselves to God. Christ will become your Mediator, and in blessing you, He will take away the guilt and curse of sin. He will purge you from it, and He will make you, through His blood, a most acceptable offering unto God. Christ will readily introduce you to Him. He will be pleased to make such a present unto God, and God Himself will be pleased to receive it.

All Your Heart

Lastly, you must give yourselves to God with all your hearts. This giving up yourselves to God must not be a mere formality, but it must be a hearty offering and devoting of yourselves to God. It must be done in the heart, and from there it must proceed, or God will not regard you. Your hearts must be given up to God, or you are not complete or sincere in your devotion to Him. And if you give up yourselves to God, without your hearts approving and concurring. Your offering is but the sacrifice of hypocrites, which is an abomination to Him.

No! Your hearts are the principal and most peculiar things that God regards, and they indeed include and contain all others. The preacher therefore, does not say the hand or head, but heart, because by the possession of the heart God has all the members of the soul and body devoted to Him. Without the heart, God values not the rest. To give to God an outward show of piety is but a mocking of Him, unless your hearts go with it. Give your hearts, and you give Him all. Give Him not your hearts, and you really give Him nothing, whatever else you seem to give Him.

Sincerity

You must be sincere and hearty. Therefore, in your giving up of yourselves, you must truly give yourselves to God. You only make an outward show, but

God beholds your secret enmity and aversion to Him. You must not only give up yourselves entirely and forever to Him, but you must also do it without reluctance. You must do it freely, and with full consent of soul. In fact, you must set your heart and highest love on God. From your highest esteem of God and your earnest desire to enjoy and serve Him, you must give yourselves unto Him.

Thus, I have briefly shown you what it is to give up your hearts to God, and you must take care to do this in your youthful age. This is your first and great and most incumbent duty. You must not allow yourselves to live an hour, no, not a moment, till you have given yourselves to God. As soon as you were capable of knowing Him, you should have given yourselves to Him, and if you have not done it yet, you must do it now, and without the least delay.

In order to convince you of this most incumbent duty, we now proceed more largely to consider those great and solemn obligations you are under to give yourselves to God in your early days.

It is very likely that many of you think that this is a matter of very great indifference. Multitudes among you seem to think so, by your lewd, ungodly lives, and by your light and vain behavior in the house of God. You seem to think as if you were not under any obligations to be religious in your youthful age. Or, at least you think that your obligations are but trifling things, and of little force and moment. Many of you seem to be entirely careless whether or not to give your hearts to God. You exceedingly neglect Him, and you rather set yourselves against Him. You give up your hearts to earthly things and pleasures, to youthful lusts and vanities, and not to God. Alas, you little think what great and solemn obligations are lying on you to devote your hearts to God in your early days!

Obligations

Your obligations are the most great and solemn that can be thought of, and if you are not obliged to give yourselves to God, you are obliged to nothing. And your obligations are so numerous that I cannot mention nor conceive them all, nor can I now express a thousandth part of those I might conceive. I can think of nothing that is not an obligation on you to be religious. Every attribute of God is an obligation on you to give yourselves unto Him. Every work of God you see presents an obligation to you. Every mercy you receive, and every affliction which you meet with, even every good and every evil of which you hear in the world. Every thing contained in the Word of God and every thing you have or are able to do for God is an obligation on you to give yourselves unto Him. But I must confine myself to a few:

There is a God, a most glorious and sovereign God and therefore, you are obliged to give your hearts unto Him in your early days.

This argument and obligation rises from the being, nature and perfections of God. And I begin with this, because it is the first foundation of all religion. Now, I need not go about to prove that there is a God. I believe you are sensible, that this glorious sun, moon and stars, and even you yourselves could not be made without Him. I will only now consider briefly who and what He is, and you will clearly see yourselves obliged to give your hearts unto Him in your early days.

He is most glorious and perfect in Himself and therefore, you are obliged to give your hearts unto Him in your early days.

Who Is God?

You have learned already that there is but one only true and living God, and that He is a Spirit of Himself, and for Himself. *"Of Himself,"* i.e., He is the first cause, He is self-existent, or He existeth lives and acts of Himself alone, and from no other. *"For Himself,"* i.e., He is the highest end, He lives and acts chiefly for Himself alone, and in subordination to Himself, for other things.

God is absolutely perfect, a most pure Spirit without body, parts, or passions, and free from all composition. You have also learned that He is infinite, eternal, and unchangeable in His being, wisdom, power, holiness, justice, goodness, and truth. God is without beginning, and He can never have an end. He is immense and omnipresent. He is always present in every place, and He always views everything present, future, past, and possible. God is omniscient also, i.e., He always sees and knows whatever has been, is, and what will come to pass. Yea, God entirely sees whatever might have been, and whatever can be. He is an all-wise and all-mighty being. He is immutably the same from everlasting to everlasting. He is independent, supreme and sovereign, self-sufficient, all-sufficient, and in Himself alone is infinitely happy.

Such a glorious Being is surely most worthy of our highest love and admiration. If any thing should be loved or admired by you for its excellency or perfections, surely God must be so. Every divine perfection is most worthy of your highest love, delight, and wonder, and every divine perfection is a great and indispensible obligation on you to give your hearts to God. I might easily show how they are, if I had the time to run into particulars. But in general, how highly should you reverence and fear Him? How profoundly should you adore and worship Him? How earnest should you be to know Him and to be acquainted with Him? How desirous should you be of the favor, love, and friendship of so great a being? How ready should you be to serve Him? And how heartily should you resign yourselves unto Him?

Oh, vain youth and children, how inexcusable is it that you should refuse your hearts to this most glorious and perfect being, and give them up to perishing and empty things and pleasures!

God is the infinite and sovereign fountain of being, life, and goodness. Therefore, you are obliged to give your hearts unto Him in your early days.

God alone is infinite in all perfections. He has an infinite source of goodness in Him. He is the only living and self-existent being and therefore, He is the infinite and sovereign fountain of being, life and goodness unto others. And as God is infinite in life and goodness, so He is infinitely bountiful and liberal. He is an eternal fountain full and overflowing, one that can never be exhausted or diminished. As God can make you to live forever, so He freely communicates eternal life unto you. He is infinitely exuberant in goodness and happiness, and He is more full and abounding in them to you than the sun itself in warmth or light unto the world.

How much are you then obliged to give your hearts to Him, who is the only infinite and sovereign fountain of life and goodness? They all depend upon His sovereign will and pleasure, and they must proceed from Him. To be sure, you all desire to live forever and be happy, and how inconsistent is it to refuse your hearts to Him from whom alone they grow?

Made for His Glory

God has made all things for His own glory and He has made you to glorify and enjoy Him forever. Therefore, you are obliged to give your hearts to God in your early days.

This argument and obligation rises from your creation and the ends of it. And surely this is the most inviolable obligation on you to give yourselves to God, from whom you have entirely received your very life and being, and that you may thereby answer the ends of them. Here are these two particulars:

God has made you and all other things, and you are therefore obliged to give your hearts to God in your early days.

We observed before, that God is the sovereign fountain of life and being and now, that He is the actual and universal Creator. Before He made the world, it entirely depended on His sovereign will and pleasure whether or not to bring it into being. But first He willed it and spoke the word and then the whole creation, in a moment, sprang from nothing. He brought this lower world into a beautiful order, and made every kind of creature in it in six days time. God is the Creator and Former of all things.

God's Absolute Right

Having therefore made all things in the world, God has an absolute right and propriety in them. They are the things of God and therefore, it is just and right that they should be improved for Him. Youth and children, you are God's by right of creation, as are all other things in the world. Surely then, you are indispensably obliged to give yourselves and all you have to God. You must be devoted to God, you must live to God, and you must improve everything for God, or else you profanely rob Him of His right and due.

Then, as the crown of all His works in this world below, He made and formed man. He formed a most beautiful body of the dust of the earth, and He breathed into it a soul, a spirit immortal. In every successive age, as the children of men have died, God has wonderfully made and raised up others. How devoutly does the psalmist admire His Creator for so glorious a work, in Psalm 139:14-18.

You are not that far removed from when you came out of the creating hands of God. O youth and children! Your very name reminds you of your late creation. We call you young, which is as much as to say you are but newly made, you are but newly come out of the hands of God. The preacher, therefore, mentions this as a peculiar obligation on you to remember God in your early days, *"Remember now your Creator in the days of your youth"* (Eccl. 12:1). It is as if He should say, your very youth should put you in mind of God. Children! Will you refuse your hearts to Him who made you almost as soon as you have come from His hands? – O base ingratitude!

The Forming Hands of God

You are even now, in some respects, in the forming hands of God. God has not brought you yet to your full maturity of either soul or body. He is now a building up your bodies every day and in a few years time, you expect He will raise you to your perfection of strength and to your highest stature. God is also gradually increasing the powers of your minds, and do you hope it will not be long before He will bring you to your strength of reason and understanding? You plainly see that God is even now forming you. He is carrying you on to the perfection of life and will you now deny Him your hearts, even while He is making you? I lack words to describe such a vile injustice, such an horrid ingratitude.

All Things for His Glory

The end of God's making all things is for His sovereign glory. The end of His making you is for you to glorify and enjoy Him forever. Therefore, you should be entirely devoted to Him.

God always acts in perfect wisdom, and before He creates or forms, He first proposes an end that moves Him. His own glory must be the sovereign end of all His works. The glory and honor of God was the ultimate design that He pursued in everything He has made. Therefore, it is one of the highest obligations on you to give up yourselves and all you have to God. Surely the great intention of God Himself in the creation of things should direct and govern you. Surely you should exactly conform to the sovereign design of Him that made them.

Remember then, that God has made all things. First for Himself and for His sovereign glory, and if you do not devote yourselves to God, you do not comply with the design of your great Creator. If you do not improve yourselves and all you have for the glory of God, you live and act in a bold opposition to His design and end in making them. You presumptuously abuse the thing of God which He has made for His glory, and you vilely pervert them from His purposes to ends of your own.

Out of Nothing

But in a peculiar manner, God has brought you out of nothing and formed you, to glorify and enjoy Him forever. This was God's great design in creating and forming you, to glorify and serve Him with the highest delight, and to enjoy Him forever. These are the two great ends of God in making and sending you into the world, and do you not think that they oblige you to mind them? Can you imagine that you may be allowed to neglect the very ends for which God has so wonderfully made you and sent you into the world? Can you dare to cross them, or live against them? Oh how hurried and heinous is this, and how incensing to your sovereign and almighty Creator!

God takes sovereign and providential care of all His works, and a particular care of you. Therefore, you ought to be devoted to God.

This argument arises from the work and design of providence. God, having created the world, He does not desert it, but He continually exercises a sovereign providence over you and everything He has made. Having brought you out of nothing and having made you to show forth His praises, God takes particular care of you that you may answer the end of your being. Children! You are under the peculiar care of providence, and you ought to be devoted to God.

Give Your Whole Heart to Him

In this care of providence, there are these things to consider:

God is your continual and entire Preserver and therefore, you should be entirely devoted to Him.

God upholds the whole creation by a constant act of His power and wisdom. This upholding, if possible, continually increases His right and interest in it. There is nothing in all this world that does not always need His supporting hand. If God withheld the exercise of His sovereign power, they would immediately vanish to nothing. God continually bears up the pillars both of heaven and earth. He continually supports and upholds them and everything in them, both in their being and order (Hebrews 1:3). They entirely depend upon God to preserve them. To be sure, He sustains them for the same reason for which He has made them. He upholds them that they may accomplish the glorious end of their almighty creation.

He Is Your Preserver

In particular, God is your great preserver. You entirely and constantly depend upon Him for the continuance of your life and being. As God has granted you life and favor, so it is His visitation that has preserved your spirit (Job. 10:12). God is your constant and supreme supporter and defender. He continually holds your souls in life and protects your lives from multitudes of evils that would soon destroy them. God has all along been your great preserver, and He now upholds you and lifts you up from sinking into nothing, death, and misery.

If God had not continually protected and upheld you, you would have long before this time gone down with multitudes of other children into the rotting grave. You would have been consumed to ashes or the worms would have been feeding on you, as they are on others. And if you have not given yourselves to God, you would now be with multitudes of other wicked children, suffering the vengeance of eternal fire.

Now consider children! How great and constant are your obligations to devote yourselves and live to God, in whom you *"live and move and have"* your being (Acts 17:28). Every hour God upholds your lives, He adds to your great and multiplied obligations. Every hour you neglect to give your hearts to God, you dreadfully increase your guilt and sin, against Him. O sinful children! How contrary do you walk to God! While God is heaping obligations on you, you are most ungratefully affronting and abusing Him. Would you have God preserve His creatures, that you may abuse them to His dishonor? Or would you have God uphold your lives, that you may sin more against Him? How inexpressibly black and horrid is this extreme ingratitude and impiety!

He Is Your Observer

God is the sovereign observer of all things, and He takes a particular notice of you. Therefore, you should be entirely devoted to Him.

God must observe the things He has made, to see if they serve the ends of His making them. He must observe if they are improved, abused, and perverted from His service and honor which He created them for.

However, the eye of God is upon the children of men. *"For the ways of man are before the eyes of the Lord, And He ponders all his paths"* (Prov. 5:21). Yea, *"the Lord weighs the hearts"* (Prov. 21:2).

O youth and children! The focused eye of God is always upon you, both to see what you want and what you do, what you have, and how you use or abuse it. God does not just see you as an unconcerned spectator, but He takes special notice of you as your Sovereign Lord.

He Does You Good

He observes your wants that He may pity you and supply them. He observes your sins and dangers, that He may warn you of them and save you from them. He observes your troubles that He may support you under and deliver you out of them. He observes your duties, that He may quicken and help you to do them. He observes your prayers, that He may give them an answer. He observes your ways, that He may bring them into judgment. He observes your obedience, that He may reward and bless you. And He observes your faults, that He may chastise and punish you (Jer. 2:19, 17:10).

The Obligation

Now children! What a great and solemn obligation is this upon you, to give up your hearts and lives to God! When the glorious and watchful eyes of God are always on you and He carefully looks both to your hearts and actions, when He views and ponders all your ways, when He looks to see how you use or abuse His creatures, He looks upon you with a gracious eye of love and favor if you be entirely devoted to Him. But He looks upon you with a dreadful eye of anger if you live and walk in your own devices.

Supreme and Sovereign Lord

God is the supreme and Sovereign Lord. You should be entirely given up to Him.

God has an absolute right to govern the things He has made, which He continually upholds by a sovereign act of His power and wisdom. He has an eternal right to give His creatures what laws He pleases, and to rule them as He sees fit. And as God has such a right, He is infinitely capable of maintaining and improving it, according to His sovereign pleasure. God therefore orders and rules the world and all things in it as He pleases. *"His kingdom rules over all"* (Ps. 103:19). And He *"works all things according to the counsel of His will"* (Eph. 1:11).

Laws Given

You are also subject to God's laws and government. God is your Sovereign Lord and King, and His sovereign will and pleasure is to control and govern you. He has given you laws to guide you in your obedience to Him, and His laws are strictly holy, just and good. *"He has shown you, O man, what is good; And what does the Lord require of you but to do justly, to love mercy, and to walk humbly with your God"* (Mic. 6:8)? As God gives you laws, so He actually rules and governs you according to His sovereign pleasure. *"He does according to His will in the army of heaven and among the inhabitants of the earth. No one can restrain His hand Or say to Him, 'What have You done?'"* (Dan. 4:35).

How strongly are you then obliged to devote yourselves and live to God? It is the highest justice that you should entirely yield obedience to His sovereign laws and government. Youth and children! Can you think yourselves exempted from the sovereign will and government of God? Can any of you think that God gives you leave to trample on His supreme authority and rebel against Him? Or can you possibly imagine that you may reject His laws, abuse His creatures, and resist Him as you please, and God not resent it? O no, vain youth! God will, sometime or other, make you dearly know that He is your Sovereign Lord and ruler, and that you will not harden yourselves against Him and go unpunished.

Sovereign Judge

Therefore, God is the righteous and sovereign Judge and Rewarder, and He will judge and repay you just as you deserve. This is yet another great and solemn obligation on you to be devoted to Him in your early days.

It is most fitting and necessary that He who made, upholds, observes, and rules the world, should also judge it. Only God knows the good and righteous ends for which He made the world, and He knows best how far they have been perverted or advanced. The great and Sovereign Lord of heaven and earth must take care to maintain the glory of His authority and power and do justice to Himself. And therefore, God must judge the world.

Similar to this, we find in Acts 17:31 that *"He has appointed a day on which He will judge the world in righteousness by the Man whom He has ordained. He has given assurance of this to all by raising Him from the dead."*

God Will Judge

Let me tell you, O youth and children! God will surely judge you with the rest of men, and He will give you your just desserts. If the judgment does not come before you die, as nothing on earth is certain but that it may come tonight, yet after death then comes the judgment (Heb. 9:27). Your souls will then immediately be judged by God, and either doomed to be bound and reserved with devils in chains of darkness or transported with the saints to paradise, 'till the resurrection of your bodies and the judgment of the great day. Then your bodies will be raised from the dead and your souls will join them. *"You will see the Son of Man sitting at the right hand of the Power, and coming on the clouds of heaven"* (Matt. 26:64). *"When the Son of Man comes in His glory, and all the holy angels with Him, then He will sit on the throne of His glory. All the nations will be gathered before Him"* (Matt. 25:31-32). *"For we must all appear before the judgment seat of Christ, that each one may receive the things done in the body, according to what he has done, whether good or bad"* (2 Cor. 5:10). The *"Son of Man will come in the glory of His Father with His angels, and then He will reward each according to his works"* (Matt. 16:17).

"And I saw the dead, small and great, standing before God, and books were opened. And another book was opened, which is the Book of Life. And the dead were judged according to their works, by the things which were written in the books. The sea gave up the dead who were in it, and Death and Hades delivered up the dead who were in them. And they were judged, each one according to his works. Then Death and Hades were cast into the lake of fire. This is the second death. And anyone not found written in the Book of Life was cast into the lake of fire" (Rev. 20:12-15).

Fear God

Oh! Youth and children! How greatly does this oblige you to devote yourselves and live to God? Oh! How subject and obedient should you be to Him that is your sovereign Judge who now observes you, that He may hereafter give you righteous judgment? You may rejoice, O young person, in your youth, and let your heart cheer you in the days of your youth and walk in the ways of your heart and in the sight of your eyes, but know that for all these things, God will bring you into judgment. Thus, the wise man tells you in Ecclesiastes 11:9 and in the last two verses of the following chapter, we hear the conclusion of the whole matter: *"Fear God and keep His commandments, for this is man's all. For God will bring every work into judgment, including every secret thing, whether good or evil"* (Eccl. 12:13-14). Also note Proverbs 24:12: *"If you say, 'Surely we did not know this,' does not He who weighs the hearts consider it? He who keeps your soul, does He not know it? And will He not render to each man according to his deeds?"*

Give Your Heart

God's wonderful grace and kindness to you is a vast and infinite obligation on you to give your hearts to Him in your early days. I might have reduced this under the last, general heading, but this kind of obligation is so notable, and so exceedingly vast and comprehensive that I think it best to be considered by itself. It contains ten thousand times ten thousand obligations in it, even as many as are your sins and mercies. Every mercy is a great engagement to you, and I might as well attempt to count the blades of grass or the sands of the seashore, as the mercies of God. But in general:

God Has Been Gracious

God has been wonderfully kind and gracious to you, and therefore, you are under the highest obligations to give up your hearts to God. God has been wonderfully kind in your very creation. God has not made you brutes, but reasonable creatures. God has made you capable of knowing, loving, serving, and enjoying Him, and of being beloved and made happy in Him forever. God has given to many of you healthy and lovely bodies, and He has given you all most precious and immortal souls. He has given you your understanding, your wit, your memory, your vivacity, your easiness to learn, your tongues, your utterance, your tunable voices; and all your other natural endowments.

Circumstances

God has also been very gracious to you in the circumstance, time, and place of your birth. God has made many of you to come of those that are virtuous and godly which is a great priviledge. Yea, God has been graciously providing for you before He ever made you. He had planted His gospel in this age of the world and in these ends of the earth, and He had brought most of your parents into the bonds of the covenant. He has made the lines to fall to you in pleasant places, and has given you a goodly heritage (Ps. 16:5-6).

Keeping You

God has been gracious to you ever since you were born. He has fed you, clothed you, nourished you, and has made you to increase and grow. He has tenderly watched over you both by night and day. He has ordered it, that most among you should have a good and happy education. He has advanced you in knowledge, understanding, learning, and, to many among you, He has graciously kept one or both of your parents alive. When they have died, He has graciously raised up friends to take care of you, to cherish, protect, advise and guide you.

Temporal Blessings

God has been wonderfully gracious in multitudes of temporal blessing and comforts. How often has God descended and saved you in the midst of dangers? How often has God delivered you from sickness and other afflictions? How many temporal benefits has He daily bestowed upon you? You know not the number. God has given to many of you the invaluable mercies of strength and health, and though you may yet be insensible of so great a privilege, yet God has granted you to live in a place of many precious civil liberties.

The Work of Christ

Above all, God has been wonderfully gracious to you in what He has done by Christ for your eternal salvation and happiness. When you were condemned, lost, and perishing sinners, God, from His astonishing and sovereign grace, has given His only and eternal Son to die to redeem you. Herein He has shown His astonishing and sovereign love, that when you were ungodly, Christ died to save you. And when Christ has died to purchase your eternal redemption, God has sent forth His spirit to convert you and bring you to it (Rom. 5:5-9).

Spiritual Advantages

God has distinguished His grace in bestowing on you a multitude of spiritual privileges and advantages of grace and eternal life. He has given you the knowledge of Christ and His glorious gospel. The things which He has hidden from multitudes of the wise and prudent of the earth, He has revealed to you. He has given you His blessed word: and to every one among you I may say as the apostle in 2 Timothy 3:15: *"From childhood you have known the Holy Scriptures, which are able to make you wise for salvation through faith which is in Christ Jesus."* God has also granted you the pure ordinances of His house and worship. God has given you most excellent catechisms, and trained you up in the most material truths of revealed religion.

Instructions and Warnings

God has sent you multitudes of instructions, warnings, councils, examples, encouragements, and corrections. He has made you hear a great many sermons. He has given you the privilege of multitudes of prayers. He has made you the offers of grace and salvation innumerable times. He has earnestly solicited you to accept and embrace them. He has often set eternal life and death before you, and urged you to the choice of eternal life and happiness. To conclude, God has given you many powerful convictions of conscience and the workings of His Holy Spirit, to open your eyes and to turn you from darkness to light and from the power of Satan to God, that you *"may receive forgiveness of sins and an inheritance among those who are sanctified by faith in Me"* (Acts 26:18).

His Care

God is still very wonderfully gracious to you, and therefore you are exceedingly obliged to give up your hearts unto Him in your youthful days. Notwithstanding all your daring sin and contempt of God, He still upholds and spares you from your deserved punishment. The devils are your malicious enemies, and as roaring lions they would fall upon you and dreadfully torment and devour you, except that God continually restrains them. Though you have constantly abused the riches of God's goodness, He continues to give them to you. You are yet the amazing monuments of His mercy, patience, and forbearance. O, that you might now be led to repentance by them!

God continues to give you multitudes of temporal blessings. You can look on nothing, you can think of nothing, but that you behold a mercy of God's bestowing. He still preserves your most precious lives, whereby you alone can enjoy and relish them. He keeps you every moment from dropping into hell while you are abusing His patience. He is filling your unthankful and unfruitful lives with a great variety and abundance of delights and comforts.

He continues to offer to you multitudes of spiritual advantages: the means of grace, the hopes of glory, His powerful restraints on many violent lusts, and the lively helps of His Spirit to enlighten, awaken, convert, and comfort you, and lead you in the way everlasting.

Eternal Happiness

God is even at this very moment using means to save you and bring you to eternal happiness. He grants you this very opportunity of hearing the things that concern your everlasting peace and welfare. He now brings me to preach the words of eternal life unto you, to you, O youth and children, and He brings you now to hear them that your souls may live.

God takes no pleasure in your death and destruction. He does not delight in your ruin and misery. He is loath to give you up and destroy you. He would rather you turn from your sins and be saved and He greatly desires it. He commands me to tell you,

"Say to them: 'As I live,' says the Lord God, 'I have no pleasure in the death of the wicked, but that the wicked turn from his way and live. Turn, turn from your evil ways! For why should you die, O house of Israel" (Ezek. 33:11)?

God Ready Call

Finally, God is ready to receive and forgive you. He is ready to be reconciled eternally to you and to enter into an everlasting covenant of grace and friendship with you. He is ready to make you His children forever, and to give you a right to all the privileges of the sons of God. He is ready to bless you with all spiritual blessings in heavenly things in Christ. He is perfectly free and ready to save you and make you happy forever. After all your heinous sins and slights of His grace and mercy, God now repeats His compassionate calls and offers to you. He invites and calls you, *"Incline your ear, and come to Me. Hear, and your soul shall live; and I will make an everlasting covenant with you—the sure mercies of David"* (Isa. 55:3).

Be Reconciled

God and Christ now entreat and urge you to be reconciled to God. God has committed to us, His ministers, the word of reconciliation. Now then, we are ambassadors for Christ. Though God did beseech you through us, we beseech you now in Christ's stead - be reconciled to God. We then, as workers together with Him, beseech you also that you do not receive His grace in vain. For He has said, *"In an acceptable time I have heard you, and in the day of salvation I have helped you. Behold, now is the accepted time; behold, now is the day of salvation"* (2 Cor. 5:19-6:2).

Not What You Deserve

All these mercies flow from God's absolutely free, sovereign, and distinguishing grace and this is a vast obligation to give up yourselves unto Him.

You do not deserve even the least of these mercies. You deserve to be entirely and forever banished from the favor of God and all His goodness. You were born full of sin and enmity to Him, and hell was your deserved portion as soon as you came into the world. Ever since you were born, you have hardly done anything else but forgotten, neglected, slighted, and rebelled against Him. You have abused His mercies, disobeyed His voice, dishonored His name, and cast His authority under your feet. Alas! You have hardly done anything else but abounding and growing in sin, repeating your affronts of your great Creator, and deserving a more severe misery. Oh! How exceedingly great are your sins and guilt under the invaluable means you have enjoyed, and how wonderful is the forbearance and long-suffering of God!

Many Mercies Extended

How distinguishing is His goodness and patience to you! How many millions of children have never enjoyed your mercies? How many millions have perished and are perishing in the heathen world? Oh, how many millions of other children are now in the grave and in hell who came into the world since you, and were not such heinous sinners, while God preserves you from going down into the pit and from the dreadful place of your torment!

Now, O children! How innumerable and vast are your obligations to be devoted to God? What could God have done more for you than He has done? Would you have Him give you heaven and glory against your wills? Why, He has sent His Son to purchase them for you. He has offered them to you. He has used all the means you can devise and more, that He might bring you to the happy possession. If you yet refuse Him your hearts, when He has done so much to deserve them, and at the same time, give them to the vile pleasures of sin or the trifles of the world, how great and inexpressible is your guilt and ingratitude? You deserve a thousand times greater punishment than Gomorrah or Sodom, and if you die in your sins, God will surely give it to you. *"I beseech you therefore, brethren, by the mercies of God, that you present your bodies a living sacrifice, holy, acceptable to God, which is your reasonable service"* (Rom. 12:1).

Your Dependence on God

You still continually and entirely depend upon God for all that is good, and therefore you are under the highest obligations to be devoted to Him.

You cannot live or subsist a moment longer without the continuance of His supporting goodness and power. You cannot have any comfort or mercy that you want, unless God bestow it. You cannot have anything that you possess continued to you, unless God continue it. You still entirely depend upon God for every mercy, both for soul and body, for time and for eternity. You still entirely and continually depend upon God, to defend and preserve you from multitudes of temporal evils, even to keep you out of hell and eternal miseries.

Surely, children! Such a state of constant and absolute dependence upon God is one of the strongest obligations. When you still continually depend upon God both for being, preservation, and happiness, for everything you lack and for everything you have, can you yet refuse to live to God? You most ungratefully and madly sin against your own happiness and mercies.

Do you not reckon it a vast obligation upon you to be devoted to your parents, because your dependence is on them to keep and support you and contrive for your comfort, and when you come of age, to give you a portion? How vastly greater is your obligation to be devoted to God your heavenly Father, when your parents, as well as yourselves, have an entire dependence upon Him both for the preservation of life, for a temporal subsistence and comfort, and for an eternal inheritance?

Your Duty

The very light of nature, reason, and natural conscience oblige you to be devoted to God. Children! You are born into the world with a sense of this great and fundamental duty. It naturally rises from the power and light of your minds, and is one of the first dictates of reason.

God Himself has set up a shining light in you to lead you to Him. The wise man therefore tells us, *"The spirit of a man is the lamp of the Lord, searching all the inner depths of his heart"* (Prov. 20:27). This spirit of man is his reasonable soul and conscience and it is the candle, or light, of the Lord. God has kindled it, inspired it, and set it up in you to show you your duty and to help you to discern and judge of yourselves and your actions. This heavenly light shows you as soon as you come to know anything of God, that you should be devoted to Him. It clearly and strongly convinces you that this is a most important and indispensable duty. When you refuse to give up yourselves unto God, this light of your conscience clearly discerns it; it shows you your wickedness, and terribly reproves and threatens you. You may often neglect it and desperately try to quench and destroy it, but it burns so strongly, that it can never be entirely extinguished. It is the faithful deputy and witness of God, the eternal judge which He has set up in your souls, and it will never utterly leave you.

Conscience Calls

Children! The very natural light of your reason and conscience oblige you, therefore, to be devoted to God. It plainly and irresistibly shows you this duty. In the name and stead of God, it peremptorily requires you to do it. It solemnly wants you to refuse it at your peril. If you are devoted to God, it approves and rejoices you, but if you keep your hearts from Him it will accuse, convince, and reprove you, and it will more or less dreadfully condemn and punish you (Rom. 2:14-15).

The Word Calls

The Word of God, which is His revealed will and law, does in a more specific manner oblige you to devote yourselves to Him.

The Word of God, as you have learned, is contained in the Holy Scriptures, and the apostle assures you, *"All Scripture is given by inspiration of God, and is profitable for doctrine, for reproof, for correction, for instruction in righteousness"* (2 Tim. 3:16). It is an express revelation of the mind and will of God concerning the children of men, and of the way of our eternal salvation and happiness. It is an abundantly clearer and fuller discovery than the light of nature can possibly yield us. God has sent it, oh children to you, and it is a vast addition to your obligations from your natural reason and conscience to be devoted to God.

O youth and children! Here is the will of the great and Sovereign God expressly revealed and proclaimed to you. Everything revealed in His Word obliges you to give yourselves to Him. It is even first revealed and written from this great end and purpose:

"For He established a testimony in Jacob, and appointed a law in Israel, which He commanded our fathers, that they should make them known to their children; that the generation to come might know them, the children who would be born, that they may arise and declare them to their children, that they may set their hope in God, and not forget the works of God, but keep His commandments" (Ps. 78:5-7).

In general, all the instructions and truths contained in the Scriptures are both a means and encouragement to lead you to God. All the counsels and exhortations in them, all the warnings and severe reproofs, all the commands and institutions, all the gracious promises and terrible threatening, all the instances both of sin and of goodness, and especially of early religion, all the examples both of judgment and mercy, and, finally, all the gracious invitations and directions that are given in Scripture, are designed as a means to bring you to God, and are great and high obligations on you to give yourselves to Him.

Give Him Your Heart

In particular, God expressly requires and calls you to give up your hearts to Him in the time of your youth. Thus it is expressly required in the text, and surely, when God has once expressly required it, that is enough to oblige you. He has declared His will, and He need say no more.

Come

However, I will mention a few more places that the revealed will and command of God may appear more clearly, and come with a stronger influence on you. *"Come, you children, listen to me; I will teach you the fear of the Lord"* (Ps. 34:11). *"Now therefore, listen to me, my children, for blessed are those who keep my ways"* (Prov. 8:32). *"You shall not delay to offer the first of your ripe produce and your juices. The firstborn of your sons you shall give to Me"* (Ex. 22:29). *"Honor the Lord with your possessions, and with the first fruits of all your increase"* (Prov. 3:9). *"But seek first the kingdom of God and His righteousness, and all these things shall be added to you"* (Matt. 6:33). *"Remember now your Creator in the days of your youth"* (Eccl. 12:1). *"My son, fear the Lord"* (Prov. 24:21).

"As for you, my son Solomon, know the God of your father, and serve Him with a loyal heart and with a willing mind; for the Lord searches all hearts and understands all the intent of the thoughts. If you seek Him, He will be found by you; but if you forsake Him, He will cast you off forever" (1 Chron. 28:9).

"Flee also youthful lusts; but pursue righteousness, faith, love, peace with those who call on the Lord out of a pure heart" (2 Tim. 2:22). *"Both young men and maidens; old men and children. Let them praise the name of the Lord, for His name alone is exalted; His glory is above the earth and heaven"* (Ps. 148:12-13).

Nothing of Greater Importance

You are under the highest obligations to give up yourselves to God because it is of the highest importance and necessity to you. There is nothing in the world of greater significance or necessity. There is nothing of greater importance to the glory and honor of God, the good and welfare of others, or your own salvation and happiness.

The glory and honor of God your Creator is highly associated with the devotion of yourselves to Him. In the very giving up of yourselves to God, you greatly honor Him, and in refusing or neglecting it, you exceedingly dishonor Him in the eyes of men and angels. A life of obedience and service whereby God is greatly glorified entirely depends upon the devoting yourselves to Him. If you resign yourselves to God, you will live to His honor, but if you refuse to give yourselves to Him, you will continue to dishonor Him and rob Him of His glory.

Welfare of Others

Like the glory and honor of God, so the good and welfare of others require and oblige you to be devoted to Him. God requires you to promote the welfare of others. If you give up yourselves to God in subjection and subordination to Him, you will be devoted to the service of men. With a holy and ardent zeal for His honor and glory, you will earnestly labor to promote their temporal and eternal welfare.

Your Own Happiness

Most importantly, devoting yourselves to God is of the greatest importance and necessity to your own salvation and happiness, children! You are by nature in a state of sin. You are condemned by God to eternal misery. You can never deliver yourselves, and if you do not give up yourselves to God through Christ, you can never be saved. There is no other way to be saved from hell and eternal misery. If this is entirely and heartily done and continued in, you shall surely be saved from them. Surely, then, this great law of necessity and self-preservation which is one of the first laws of nature, obliges you to be devoted unto God. Unless you give yourselves to God, you can never be happy, for you can never have a share in His favor, and you can never enjoy Him, who is the only suitable and perfect happiness, and satisfactory portion.

Pleasing to Heavenly Hosts

You are under the highest obligation to be devoted to God, because it is most highly pleasing, both to God, angels, and men.

Being devoted to God is most highly pleasing to God, for in this you obey and honor Him. You are to be saved and happy, to do good in the world, and to answer the great ends of your being. God beholds you with singular delight and pleasure. He highly approves, esteems and commends you, and He very dearly loves you. *"I love those who love me, and those who seek me diligently will find me"* (Prov. 8:17).

Again, it is most highly pleasing to the glorious angels. Those pure and heavenly creatures are most entirely devoted to God. They are perfectly happy in their conformity to Him, and they exquisitely desire and delight to see you so, too. They are extremely displeased at your living without God in the world, but when you repent and give yourselves to Him, the glad tidings are carried to heaven, and *"there is joy in the presence of the angels of God over one sinner who repents"* (Luke 15:10).

Pleasing to Men

This is also most highly pleasing to the best and greatest of men. King David himself esteemed the saints to be the most excellent in the earth, and in them was his highest earthly delight (Ps. 16:3). The divine apostle tells the elect lady, as so will all your pious ministers speak to your parents: *"I rejoiced greatly that I have found some of your children walking in truth, as we received commandment from the Father"* (2 John 4).

To be sure, your early devotion to God will be exceedingly delightful to your religious and solicitous parents. It will be their great honor and joy, and your neglect of piety will be their most sensible disgrace and sorrow. *"A wise son makes a glad father, but a foolish son is the grief of his mother"* (Prov. 10:1).

Pleasing to God

Children! Your early piety will be abundantly pleasing both to God, angels, and men, as your continuing in sin extremely offends them. This therefore, highly obliges you to be devoted to God.

Grace

Descending from sinful parents, you were conceived into sin, you were born in iniquity, and brought forth in pollution and sorrow. You were sinful, impure, and loathsome in the eyes of God. You were the children of wrath, and condemned to hell. You were in a perishing and helpless estate, and if you had died in that state, you would have been miserable forever. It is a wonderful grace of God that when you were vile, abominable, and sinful wretches, and could do nothing for His service, He was free to receive you into a gracious covenant and take you into His particular care.

A Kind Father

O children! God has graciously taken care of you. He has dealt as a kind Father to you. He has nourished and kept you. He has guided and brought you to years of choice and discretion. He has brought you to this present occasion. He offers you eternal life and happiness. He repeats the offer. He moves you to embrace it.

Profaning His Covenant

If you refuse to give up your hearts to this covenant God, you most wickedly violate and profane His covenant. You cast down His honor with contempt on the ground. As you unhappily forfeit the great and desirable blessings of this most excellent covenant, so you miserably entail on yourselves the dreadful execrations and curses that are denounced against the violators of it. For your awakening, I desire you to read those awful chapters, Deuteronomy 28-29, where you will see most vividly the solemn obligations you are under to keep the covenant of God.

Prayers of Friends

The desires, labors, prayers, and expectations of your pious friends and relatives are vast obligations on you to give up yourselves to God in the days of your youth.

Conviction of Conscience

Lastly, your knowledge of all these things, the inculcations of them on you, the convictions of your conscience, and the strivings of the Holy Spirit of God pose yet further obligations on you.

Though your obligations are innumerable, I must draw to a close. I will only briefly represent the particular obligations you are under to give up yourselves immediately to God in the days of your youth, without any delay, and so come to a conclusion.

Here I must tell you that the service of God is the very design of your beings, and of all your mercies. It is, therefore, the constant and whole work of your lives. All these obligations are now and always upon you, to oblige you now as much as ever to be devoted to God. Until you give up yourselves to God, you therefore live and continue in the sinful violation of them all, a daring opposition and rebellion against Him. You thereby dreadfully grow in your guilt and wickedness, and increase the wrath and curse of God upon you.

Avoid Evil

Your early devotion to God is necessary to prevent and avoid abundance of sin and evil, and to obtain and do abundance of good in the world. The present life is the only space or season of giving up yourselves to God, and the time of youth and even this very day may be your only opportunity. The spring and prime of your lives is certainly the fittest and most suitable season, the most easy and pleasant for you, and most honorable and delightful to God.

Urgency

Lastly, if you now refuse to give up yourselves to God, there is the greatest danger and likelihood that you never will do it, but go on in your sin, grow more averse to religion, and dreadfully increase your guilt in this world and your eternal doom and torment in the other.

From all these considerations and reasons, you are indispensably obliged both in duty, interest, and wisdom, to devote yourselves immediately to God in the days of your youth, and without any delay.

I have but a few reflections, and then I will be finished:

Those of Younger Age

For those that are of a younger age – oh how great, how exceeding great must then be your sin and wickedness, if, after all this, you refuse to be devoted to God! How exceedingly great and extreme is your folly and madness! How inexpressibly severe will be your future punishment! Oh! How many millions of great obligations do you contemptuously sin against and violate! Every one of them is a fearful and higher aggravation of your guilt and misery.

Those of Older Age

What an awakening word this is to those that are of a more advanced age, and yet have never given up themselves to the God that has made and preserved them! Every moment of your lives, you have proceeded in the breach of all these great obligations. Oh! What an inconceivable measure and height of iniquity have you risen into by this time! While you have refused to be devoted to God, you have never done one acceptable thing to Him in all your lives. You have been doing nothing else all this while, but continually sinning against Him. And oh! What dreadful stores of wrath you have treasured up to yourselves *"in the day of wrath and revelation of the righteous judgment of God, who will render to each one according to his deeds"* (Rom. 2:1-6).

For Everyone

For us all, and to conclude: Let us then continually remember the many great and solemn obligations we are always lying under to be devoted to God. We are His own already, by ten thousand times ten thousand obligations. If we have refused to give up ourselves to Him, we have most wickedly violated and sinned against them all. And oh! How prodigiously vast and amazing is the sin! God Himself even seems to be astonished at it, *"Hear, O heavens, and give ear, O earth! For the Lord has spoken: 'I have nourished and brought up children, and they have rebelled against Me'"* (Isa. 1:2).

Can there be a greater, a more complete and comprehensive, a more heinous and provoking sin? Yet, alas, there is this one greater than all, and that is your persisting in the sin. By persisting in your refusal to be devoted to God, you do daringly justify all your past sins in the sight of God and the world and every moment you persist in your sins, you implicitly approve them. You repeat their commission, and so continually redouble the guilt of your sins and the weight of your punishment.

Oh then, let us seriously think upon those awful words in Proverbs 1:20-33 and delay not a moment longer, but now, let us immediately give up ourselves with our hearts to God, and faithfully serve Him, for then we will enjoy Him forever. Amen.

6

the PECULIAR ADVANTAGES *of* EARLY PIETY

Mr. John Webb, Boston, May 3, 1721

Proverbs 8:32
Now therefore, listen to me, my children, for blessed are those who keep my ways.

I will endeavor at this time, by the help of God, is to set before our young people the peculiar benefits and advantages of early piety. You have already heard the various branches of duty excellently explained unto you, and your obligations unto it are strongly instilled. That therefore, which offers itself next to our consideration is the singular benefits and advantages of remembering our great Creator in the days of our youth. And as this has fallen to my lot, I have made choice of these words of divine wisdom as an introduction to the present discourse. They are found among the Proverbs of Solomon, the son of David, the king of Israel.

Book for Youth

The general design of this book was to form the manners of youth, or to teach them early how to fear and serve God aright. Proverbs is where their highest wisdom and happiness consists, so I take this to be the more particular design of the words now read unto you. This seems to be very evident from the manner in which they are delivered. *"Now therefore, listen to me, my children"* (Prov. 8:32). These words are the words of divine wisdom, or the words of Jesus Christ, the essential wisdom of the Father, *"in whom are hidden all the treasures of wisdom and knowledge"* (Col. 2:3.) And they are spoken to children, chiefly to those that are children in years, as well as in understanding.

Blessed Duty

The Proverbs contain an earnest exhortation to the most important duty, backed with the most forcible motive that could be thought of. The duty you are exhorted unto is to hearken now to the voice of your great Savior. In other words, you are to learn those lessons of early piety that you have been already instructed in, and learn them now, today, and instantly, without making one moment's delay in this matter of infinite concern. The singular encouragement you have unto the duty is a most gracious promise of blessedness in case of obedience, as in the words to be insisted on, for *"blessed are those who keep my ways"* (Prov. 8:32). The original word in this place for *"blessed,"* is a most comprehensive term, and as critics observe, includes all kind of happiness in it.

Hence, the meaning of these words is that all those who hearken to the voice, or keep the commandments of their great God and Savior from their youth up, will be blessed in every way by Him. They will be blessed with all outward blessings as far as is needful for them, but especially with all spiritual blessings, in heavenly places in Christ Jesus. They will be blessed both in their souls and in their bodies. They will be blessed in this life, at death, and forever in the world that is to come. They will be very remarkably blessed in all these and similar respects. This, children, is the glorious encouragement you have from these words of your Savior, to be religious now, in the days of your youth.

DOCTRINE
All those who hearken to the voice of Christ or become truly pious and religious in their childhood and youth are, and shall be happy and blessed in a very exclusive and distinguishing manner.

Or, more briefly:
The early convert has many very exclusive and distinguishing privileges and advantages belonging to him.

This I will endeavor, in a very plain and familiar language, show that several of those blessed privileges and advantages are, and will be, the distinguishing crown, glory, and happiness of the early convert. I say, *"several"* of these benefits and advantages, for it is impossible for me, or for any man living, to say how many, or how great and excellent they are.

I will therefore only select a few of the most remarkable of them, and enlarge upon them as time will allow.

Here, I earnestly call upon you, the young people of this numerous assembly, to give your present and most serious and devout attention, for I am now speaking unto you in the name of the Lord, and I hope, in His fear, and with a most tender concern for the eternal salvation of your precious and immortal souls. What I have to offer unto you, may, if carefully attended to, prove instrumental, by the grace of God, to instill high and honorable thoughts of early religion in you, and so be a happy means to persuade you to the present and most delightful exercises of it.

Your Happiness at Stake

Happiness, no doubt, is the mark you are aiming at. Your sprightly, vigorous, and active powers are in the full pursuit of such things that you hope to reap substantial profits and pleasures by possessing. Your thoughts and contrivances, your labors and endeavors are that your lives may prove a most delightful scene unto you. When the striving Spirit of God is at work on your tender consciences and you begin to entertain any serious thoughts about your souls and another life, you are ready to flatter yourselves presently with the hopes of complete eternal happiness in the world to come.

Now I hope, by the help of grace, to make it evident that a life of true religion entered upon and preserved in from your youth up, will more effectually answer all your rational and immortal desires for happiness than any other methods you can propose or prosecute. There is no other course of life attended with so many high and honorable, so many peculiar and distinguishing advantages as this is. But before I enter into the particulars of this most delightful subject, I will lay a foundation to all the rest, and briefly observe in general that:

By an early conversion to God, you will come early into the covenant of His grace, and so soon obtain a right and title to all the great and invaluable privileges that are contained in it. Every sinner, from the first moment of his true conversion, is taken into covenant with God, that is in all things, well ordered and sure. Now this covenant comprehends all possible blessings in it. It includes all things that pertain to life and godliness, everything that is needful for your present support and comfort, and all that is necessary to render you completely and eternally blessed in the world to come. God has graciously promised His covenant servants, (and He will be as good as His word), that He will give grace and glory, and no *"good thing will He withhold from those who walk uprightly"* (Ps. 84:11). This happiness is experienced by all the saints of the Lord, but the early convert enjoys it with a remarkable emphasis. The new convert comes first into the possession of happiness, which is a signal favor of God unto him, and, besides all the distinguishing privileges of it, it falls to his happy lot and portion. This you will plainly see, as I name the many particulars unto you.

Advantages

I will begin with the special benefits and advantages of early religion in this life and world. These I will consider, both in outward regards, and in inward and spiritual respects.

Outward Advantages

Early religion is frequently attended with many outward privileges and advantages in this life. The apostle Paul observes unto us, that *"godliness is profitable for all things, having promise of the life that now is and of that which is to come"* (1 Tim. 4:8). In these words, He refers to that promise of our blessed Savior, that we are to *"seek first the kingdom of God and His righteousness, and all these things shall be added to you"* (Matt. 6:33). All these things, food and raiment and the other necessaries and conveniences of life, spoken of in the preceding context, are implied. Though this promise of outward blessings as the reward of obedience is not, perhaps, so large and extensive in these gospel days as it was under the Old Testament dispensation, we may reasonably expect from now on to be, in some way or another, gainers by godliness - even in outward regards. The early convert has the fairest prospect of any before Him, to be a gainer by it in these two respects.

A Good Name

By being religious early, you take the most proper and direct course you can to get to establish a good name, credit, and reputation in the world, among all those whose value and esteem is worth having. True piety imparts a real glory to those that embrace it. It inspires them with such noble principles and virtues that are the distinguishing honor and ornament of those that have them.

Grace is beautiful in all, but it is eminently more so in those who are godly from a young age. It appears more pure and unmixed in them. For they have not so many of the scandalous outbreakings of sin and corruption to tarnish and eclipse the glory of it, as those that make longer delays in religion usually have.

A Crown

Therefore, it is the crown and laurel of the youth. It makes his face to shine beyond all the charms of the most ruddy complexion, and is a greater ornament unto Him than the richest pearls, or the most costly array.

Hence, all those who know how to prize and value men and things according to their true worth will account you the excellent in the earth. Your names will be valued by all the wise, good, sober and virtuous men that will have any knowledge of you. While the vain and extravagant youth is the shame of his age and the grief of all that have the best interests at heart, your godly and wise rulers and ministers, your pious and prudent parents and neighbors will look upon you with pleasure and delight.

A Treasure

Such precious sons of Zion, as you will then be, will, in their esteem, be comparable to fine gold, and they will account you the riches and glory of your country. As they see you grow up and improve in grace and virtue, they will look upon you as the hope of future time and so be able to die with greater comfort, knowing that they will be succeeded by those who are likely to do worthily in their day and generation. This is the honor you will have from the saints. Then, as to the rest of mankind, though their credit and esteem is not so much to be regarded, yet those who have any of the remains of morality in them cannot but revere that sobriety, temperance, wisdom, prudence, justice, and meekness that will adorn your conduct in the world.

Hatred of the World

Even the most profligate wretches upon earth have left not only religion, but even moral honesty itself, and are ready upon all other occasions to express their hatred against you and the ways of godliness. Yet, if they have any important affair to manage, that requires the exercise of moral virtues, such as prudence, justice, integrity, or fidelity in those they trust it with, they would sooner commit it into your hand than into the hands of their merry companions that are as equally vicious as themselves.

This is a plain evidence that undisguised virtue commands secret respect wherever it appears. *"Good understanding gains favor"* (Prov. 13:15). Now, such an established reputation in the world is the greatest of all outward advantages. It will put many opportunities into your hands to do and enjoy good here which otherwise you will certainly miss. Hence it is, as Solomon truly observes unto us, *"A good name is to be chosen rather than great riches, loving favor rather than silver and gold"* (Prov. 22:1).

Good Things

Those that are virtuous early have the most rational prospects before them of coming to the possession and enjoyment of a sufficiency of the good things of this life. There is not only a moral but natural tendency in the exercise of many Christian virtues, to get and secure to ourselves as much of this world as our state and circumstances in it may call for.

Wealth

Solomon observes unto us in Proverbs 10:4 that *"He who has a slack hand becomes poor, but the hand of the diligent makes rich."* Then by moderate spending, temperance, frugality, and the same, the virtuous man keeps what the idle spendthrift prodigally throws away. The length of days are said to be in the right hand of wisdom, so are riches and honor said to be in her left hand (Prov. 3:16). But suppose the covetous worldling should, by his extreme penny-pinching, or by sparing more than is appropriate, by cunning and theft, by bribery, extortion, cheating, and similar evil courses, amass to himself a larger possession then you are ever likely to come fairly to, yet herein you will undoubtedly have the advantage of him.

That is, you will have a better right and title to the little you lawfully possess. You will not only have a natural or civil title unto it (which is more than the cheating miser has), but you have a covenant right and title unto it, which is more than any wicked man has to the least of his enjoyments. For godliness, has the *"promise of the life that now is and of that which is to come"* (1 Tim. 4:8) and you will have the best title to what you possess.

Enjoyment

So, your enjoyment, which is the end of possession, will be more sweet and pleasant. You will not have those stings of conscience, which usually attend an ill-gotten estate and a guilty mind, to eat away at the comfort of what you have. Besides, it is likely you may be favored with a more healthy constitution, which is the very soul of all outward enjoyment, for temperance and frugality are friends to the health of the body, while intemperance, unchastity, beastly sensuality, and luxury disorder the frame of nature, corrupt the juices of the body, consume the flesh, waste the spirits, breed loathsome diseases, and so either cut short the days, or fill them up with pain and anguish.

Rich in Faith

To these I will add that the religious man has the peculiar blessing of God upon all his outward possessions, whether greater or fewer. If there is anything real to be enjoyed in them, the saint will have the comfort of them if God sees it to be best for him. Hence the psalmist assures us, *"A little that a righteous man has is better than the riches of many wicked"* (Ps. 37:16). After all, suppose you should be reduced to the lowest circumstances in the world, and have nothing that you can call your own in it, as it has sometimes been the case with very eminent saints. We read of such as are poor in this world, but rich in faith (James 2:5). I say, suppose this should be your case.

Yet, by being strictly religious, you will find your account even in this life. God will give you contentment with your outward state and condition. He that is contented in this reaps the proper fruit of possession and enjoys himself with far more ease and freedom, though he lie with Lazarus at the gate, than a wicked ruler can do, in his rich apparel, faring sumptuously every day.

Happiness

Thus, children, you see that even in outward respects, the early convert has the most rational prospects before him of being the happiest man, even in this life and world. I have rather enlarged upon this topic because the one great objection which young people have against early piety is a groundless conceit that, as soon as they become truly pious and virtuous, they must instantly abandon all that is pleasant in this world. If you will but impartially consider what has been said, it may serve to convince you that the early convert takes the most proper and rational course of any to lead a quiet, peaceable, and happy life, even in this world.

But now, these outward advantages are of least importance in the saint's inventory. There are innumerable other privileges and advantages you will obtain a title unto by the early dedication of yourselves unto God, the least of which, if laid in the balance, would weigh down this whole world, with all that is desirable in it. These are the benefits I will now direct my thoughts unto.

Early religion is attended with many peculiar spiritual privileges and advantages in this life. All who devote and give up themselves to God in their childhood and youth shall, from this time forward, be invested with all spiritual blessings in the heavenly places in Christ Jesus. To note a few instances, here are some of these inestimable distinguishing privileges.

Early Adoption

The early convert is blessed with an early adoption into the number of God's children. Every one that is renewed and sanctified by the Spirit of God immediately becomes a son, a child of God by a most gracious adoption. *"But as many as received Him, to them He gave the right to become children of God, to those who believe in His name"* (John 1:12). Hence, those that are first converted unto God have the peculiar honor to be first invested with this privilege. How great the dignity and advantage this will appear if we briefly consider what it is to become a child of God and what distinguishing privileges such are favored with.

Briefly, to become a child of God is to be taken into the nearest relationship to God that any creature is capable of. The most glorious angels in heaven have no higher title than to be called the sons of God (Job 38:7). Nay, to be called the son of God in an appropriate sense, to be the only begotten Son of God, His well-beloved Son, or the Son of His love, is the most intimate and exalted relationship that the second person in the ever-blessed Trinity stands in unto God the Father. How amazing then is the infinite condescension of the great God towards such sinful, polluted worms of the dust as we are, that He should advance us to the dignity of children by a gracious adoption! It is an honor done us, that simply considered, is infinitely greater than if we had been born of a David, of a Solomon, or of any of the most splendid monarchs that ever swayed a scepter in this world.

Changed

Again, to become a child of God is to be made like unto God. By a gracious adoption you will have the image of the heavenly Adam vividly stamped upon you (1 Cor. 15:49), that image of His which consisteth in *"righteousness and holiness"* (Eph. 4:24). This image you will be changed into, even as by the Spirit of the Lord, until at length you shall perfectly be transformed into His likeness, as far as your nature and capacity will allow (cf. 1 Cor. 3:18; 1 John 3:2). How glorious is the dignity of this! To bear a resemblance to earthly majesty makes a splendid appearance in the eyes of the world, but unspeakably more glorious in the eyes of God, angels and good men, is the least saint, being made *"partakers of the divine nature"* (2 Pet. 1:4).

Conformity to Christ

Those that are the children of God are the followers of their great God and Savior, and imitate Him in all His imitable perfections (Eph. 5:1). This is the most noble and divine life that can possibly be led by us. Since God is the origin of all excellency and perfection, so a conformity to His blessed image and example will exceedingly refine our nature, and vastly exalt us above the common level of mankind. Thus you see what it is to become a child of God, and how honorable the relationship is.

His Compassion

Now, the distinguishing privileges of it are no less wonderful and glorious. For by being a child of God, you have His fatherly compassions always extended towards you. *"As a father pities his children, so the Lord pities those who fear Him"* (Ps. 103:13). His watchful eye will ever be upon you, His tender care over you, and His bountiful hand open unto you. You may repair unto Him at all times as children to their father. You may make Him your refuge in every time of trouble, you may open all your wants and griefs unto Him, you may cast all your burdens upon Him, and beg all needful supplies from Him. All this you may do with the liberty and freedom of children, and be assured, that His ear will ever be open to your requests. For *"The eyes of the Lord are on the righteous, and His ears are open to their cry"* (Ps. 34:15).

To these I will add, by virtue of your adoption, you will obtain an unalienable right and title to the inheritance of children, a heavenly inheritance, the inheritance of the saints in light. That which will be the crown and glory of all is that you will be made a joint heir with Christ of this inheritance. *"The Spirit Himself bears witness with our spirit that we are children of God, and if children, then heirs—heirs of God and joint heirs with Christ"* (Rom. 8:16-17). These things I have but just named unto you. However, by these hints you see what the dignity and benefit of adoption is. Well then might the apostle John break forth into those admiring expressions, at the consideration of it, *"Behold what manner of love the Father has bestowed on us, that we should be called children of God"* (1 John 3:1)!

Pardon and Peace

By an early conversion to God you will be the first in obtaining pardon, peace, and reconciliation with God in and through Christ. A person is no sooner converted from the error of his ways to the wisdom of the just, but he obtains the free remission of all his iniquities. The debt that he owed to divine justice is now paid, his bonds cancelled, and an act of indemnity passed upon him. Hence you read, *"There is therefore now no condemnation to those who are in Christ Jesus, who do not walk according to the flesh, but according to the Spirit"* (Rom. 8:1).

Being thus justified from the guilt of all his sins, he obtains peace and reconciliation with God. His former enmity against God is now in a great measure removed, and God's anger turned away from him. Therefore, from hence forward, we hear the blessed proclamation of peace between them as, *"Therefore, having been justified by faith, we have peace with God"* (Rom. 5:1). This peace is brought about and concluded only in and through the Lord Jesus Christ, as in the place but now mentioned. Hence it is, Christ is called our peace (Eph. 2:14), and we are said to obtain forgiveness through His blood *"according to the riches of His grace"* (Eph. 1:7), and to be reconciled by His death, (Col. 1:21-22).

The Impact of Sin

This pardon, peace, and reconciliation are unspeakable privileges to all that are in the happy possession of it. This will appear, if you do but consider on the one hand, what a dreadful thing it is to lie under the guilt of all your sins, and so both to be an enemy to God, and to have Him for your incensed adversary. Every such sinner is under the wrath and curse of God, and so made liable to all miseries in this life, to death itself, and to the pains of hell forever. He is liable to vindictive horrors of conscience in this world, and to endless, insupportable vengeance in the world to come.

On the other hand, the greatness of this privilege will appear if you but consider what the happy effects of pardon and reconciliation with God are. These are peace in a man's own conscience, an interest in the favor of God which is better than life, and a sure title to eternal salvation.

Redemption

The pardon of sin has obtained the name *"redemption"* (Eph. 1:7). Hence, the pardoned man is expressly called a blessed man, *"Blessed is he whose transgression is forgiven, whose sin is covered. Blessed is the man to whom the Lord does not impute iniquity, and in whose spirit there is no deceit"* (Ps. 32:1-2).

Children, since pardon, peace, and reconciliation with God are such a blessed advantage to all that have an interest in them, it must be an additional privilege to come early into the possession of them. By this means, you will enjoy more of the happy fruits of them and for a longer time than others. You will have your pardon to show, while other vain youth carry about their chains of guilt with them. You will be able to call God your Father and Friend, while they cannot but look upon Him as their Enemy and Avenger. Your title to heaven will be secure, while their title is to seek. While they hang over the lake that burns with fire and brimstone by the slender thread of life, only you will have a crown of glory in reserve for you. In a word, there is nothing now but this momentary life that can stand between you and the perfection of happiness. Now judge how great this privilege of early conversion is.

The Degredation of Sin

Another present advantage of an early dedication to God is that you will hereby escape innumerable sins, snares, temptations, and sorrows that others unavoidably involve themselves in. You all know that childhood and youth are said to be vanity (Eccl. 11:10). There is no age of mankind more prone to sin or show more of sinful levity than youth, nor is there any age encompassed with more ensnaring temptations than this age. Therefore, when the young man gives loose to his corruptions, and walks in the ways of his heart, and in the sight of his own eyes, you see what fearful work he quickly makes of it. He runs into the way of every temptation, and his feet are presently entangled in the snares that Satan lays for him. He has no bridle upon his lusts, and therefore gives himself over unto lasciviousness, to work all uncleanness with greediness.

Unerasable Consequences of Sin

There is no sin so infamous, so vile, or disgraceful, but you may often behold the young person, void of understanding, vigorously pursing and practicing it. By this means he many times brings a blot upon his name which he can never wipe off in this world, and always dreadfully dishonors the name of God, grieves his pious parents and friends, and makes the most amazing work for a later repentance. Therefore, if ever the profligate wretch is brought to a true sense of the evil of his ways, and so obtains the mercy of God after he has wasted away the best of his days in sin and vanity, his repentance is usually attended with unspeakably more grief and sorrow and anguish of soul. His bones are broken and his heart deeply wounded with the sins of his youth. These make him to go mourning and limping to his grave.

But, an early conversion to God will, by divine grace, prove a most effectual remedy against all these evils. It will fill you early with hatred of sin, it will make you watchful against temptations, and when you are assaulted by them it will enable you to say with that gracious and renowned young man, *"How then can I do this great wickedness, and sin against God"* (Gen. 39:9)? Thus, by escaping the sins of youth, you will prevent the doleful sorrow and agonies of a late repentance for them. This advantage, though only a negative one, is worth more than all the positive blessings this world can afford. It is the singular happiness of an early, serious, and devout dedication to God.

Delight

By entering betimes into the service of God, you will find the duties of religion more easy, sweet, and delightful unto you than you ever could have imagined them to be. There is, indeed, a great deal of labor, pains, and cost to be expended in a life of religion. Many of the duties of it are attended with uncommon difficulty. They are directly contrary to flesh and blood. There is nothing our corrupt nature revolts more at, than at the thoughts of them. Such are the duties of self-denial, bearing the cross, of forgiving and loving our enemies, and the like.

The way to heaven is compared to a straight gate and a narrow way. Hence it is, we are called upon to strive, even to agony, that we may enter in it (Luke 13:24). However, the service is not so difficult, but there is a real pleasure and delight to be met with in it.

Great Reward

The work many times carries its own wages in it. The psalmist observes that in keeping God's commands *"there is a great reward"* (Ps. 19:11). The early convert bids the fairest of any for this reward in duty, for as he that sets out late in the service of God and begins his work either at the sixth or ninth or eleventh hour, has a great deal more work to do and less time to do it in, more numerous and powerful lusts to subdue, and less measures of grace to make headway against them. These individuals are frequently seen to drive on more heavily in their work than others. The service of God which should be their delight is too much a toil and a burden unto them.

Heart Enlarging

However, the early convert loses comparatively little of his time. He begins his work in the morning of his day, and by a diligent prosecution of it, he adjusts himself to the service of Christ. This, by the grace of God, renders the yoke of Christ easy and His burden light unto him. Custom in duty habituates it unto him. What is habitual is easy and pleasant unto us. He that sets out first in the service of God usually runs the ways of God's commands with a more enlarged heart.

Pleasantness and Peace

He finds the ways of wisdom to be ways of pleasantness, and all her paths to be peace. He takes inexpressible delight in the most difficult duties of christianity, and can deny himself, take up the cross, forgive an enemy, with greater cheerfulness than others have, who to gratify their sensual desires and appetites.

In a word, by a long course of obedience to the commandments, it will become your meat and drink, to do the will of your heavenly Father. And now, children, this is an advantage highly worth seeking after, and will unspeakably more than repay your early diligence in the work of your Lord.

Holiness Cultivated

The early convert is likely to make the richest improvements in grace and holiness. As natural habits are confirmed and strengthened by repeated acts, so are the gracious habits of a sanctified mind. Hence, the sooner you begin the exercise of grace, the more time you are likely to improve in it. If you are but industrious in this improvement you will quickly find, that as your days are multiplied, your graces will be thriving. They will, every day, grow more lively and vigorous and active in you. You will hereby obtain a more complete and entire victory over your unruly lusts and corruptions. The longer you maintain the war against them, provided you are vigilant and resolute in it, the less headway they will be able to make against you, and the less disturbance will you meet with from them.

Weakening Sin

By a constant leveling at the root of sin, the habits of it will, by degrees, grow weaker and weaker in you. Hence, many that at their first setting out in the ways of God, have found their wicked lusts and passions very exorbitant and unruly, have, by the grace of God, in continuance of time, brought them into very great subjection. Their towering pride has been battered down into the lowest humility. Their raging anger, that was wont to furiously break bounds upon every frivolous occasion, has been softened down into a dove-like meekness, and this under the highest personal affronts. Their revengeful spirit has been melted down into the most kind and benevolent temper, and their selfish disposition changed into the most self-denying frame, and so with respect to every other vile lust and affection.

Then, as to the several graces of the Spirit, by long experience and diligence in the work and service of God, exceedingly grow and improve, strengthening and increasing themselves. Your faith, which at first appears but weak and tottering and ready to fail upon every new difficulty or temptation, will by long experience and exercise grow more fixed and steady, more uniform and lively in exerting itself upon the proper objects of it, and so upon trial will be found unto praise and honor and glory, like Abraham by being strong in faith gave glory to God. Your slender hopes will, by the same means, strengthen and increase and become as an anchor, sure and steadfast cast within the veil.

Love and Delight

Your love to, and delight in, God and Christ and the things of His kingdom, will kindle into a holy flame, and become more vigorous and active by a frequent meditation upon those glorious objects, and by the larger experience you will have of the divine goodness unto you. Your filial fear and reverence of God will increase by your more frequent and near approach to His most awful sacred majesty. Your submissions to the divine will, the more often they are made, the more lowly and entirely will they prove. Your patience, by frequent exercise under trials, will at length come to have its perfect work. So may it be said of every other grace - the more time you improve, and the more often you are in the exercise of it, the more you will strengthen the habit and invigorate the several actings of it.

Thus, if God will save you while young, you are likely to be the greatest proficience in the school of Christ, to make the largest improvements in grace and holiness, and by this means to grow up to strong men in Christ Jesus, while others that set out later in the day will remain but babes in Christ. This is another singular privilege of early conversion, and a mighty encouragement to it.

More Glory for Him

The sooner you begin in the service of God, the more work you are likely to do for Him, and so bring the greater revenue of glory to His name. The glory of God is the great end for which we were all made. Since this was the principal end of your being, it must be your highest wisdom, perfection, and happiness to answer it in the best manner you can. For the glory of any creature is to answer the original design of it. Now the most effectual course you can take toward this is to begin early in the service of God, and to persevere with diligence in it.

More Opportunity

Observe, if you do but devote yourselves to God in your childhood and youth, God will put many opportunities into your hands to serve Him which He will not favor others with, and He will help you to improve many more which vain youth forever carefully let slip. By this means you will become plants of renown in the vineyard of God, and the longer He spares you in it, the more precious fruits of righteousness will you bring forth which are by Jesus Christ to the praise and glory of God. What a distinguishing crown of honor this will be upon your heads! It will render you lovely and desirable in the eyes of your great God and Savior.

Favor from God

Lastly, by setting out early in the service of God, you will experience more of the special favor of God, and of the substantial comforts of true religion while you live. God has indeed an astonishing love for all who are conformed in any good degree, to the image of His Son, but He seems to have a very peculiar distinguishing affection for all those that seek and serve Him from their youth up. This is plainly intimated unto us in those words of divine wisdom, *"I love those who love me, and those who seek me diligently will find me"* (Prov. 8:17).

Our blessed Redeemer gave no small proof of this when He fixed upon John, the youngest of all His disciples, as His beloved disciple (see John 21:7). Your great Savior, if you seek Him early, will suffer you with John to lean upon His bosom, while others will be honored only with the privilege of sitting at the table with Him. He will take you more frequently into the chambers of His delight, and show you more of the riches and honors of His kingdom. He will give you greater quiet and tranquility in your own minds, and a more established peace in your consciences.

Comfort

He will multiply the comforts of the Holy Spirit unto you, and so anoint you with the oil of joy and gladness above your fellows. You will sit under the shadow of your Savior with greater delight, and His fruit will be sweeter to your taste. You will enjoy it more abundantly, and for a longer season than others. In a word, by devoting yourselves early to the fear and service of God, you will make wonderful improvements in a life of communion with God, and so reap the first fruits of the heavenly Canaan in greater plenty while you are here in the wilderness below.

And now, dear children, what a glorious privilege is this? Do not you account it your honor and happiness to be the darlings of your earthly parents? Is not a special interest in their love, and their constant smiles upon you reckoned among the greatest of your earthly comforts? They are certainly thus esteemed by every dutiful and obedient child. But what is all this to an interest in the more exclusive love of God, and the more abundant joys of the Holy Spirit? Is not one smile from our heavenly Father infinitely more to the pious soul than all the happiness this world can afford? How transcendent then is the dignity and happiness of being His children?

Thus, upon the whole, you may plainly see that a life spent in the service of God is the most profitable and pleasant life in the whole world. Consequently, those who begin and end the day of life with God, make the best and wisest provision for themselves in time, as well as to all eternity. Thus, I have considered several of the special benefits and advantages of early religion in this present evil life and world.

Advantage at Death

I proceed now, more briefly to show what the singular advantages of early piety are likely to be in a dying hour. Death, as you are aware, is advancing quickly towards us all, towards those of you that are in your childhood and youth, as well as towards those that are of riper years. We read in Genesis 3:19: *"For dust you are, and to dust you shall return."* According to this decree, the apostle, asserts in Hebrews 9:27: *"And as it is appointed for men to die once."*

What man therefore, is he that lives and will not see death? Death is thus unavoidable and is attended, at the same time, with the utmost of natural horrors, as every one knows that has had any realizing apprehensions concerning it. I say, since it is thus, it must be a point of the highest wisdom in us to think seriously of the evil day before it comes, and to make the speediest and best provision against it that we can, so that when we come to encounter death, the prospect of it may not affright us into everlasting horror and despair.

Overcoming Fear at Death

Now the most proper course you can possibly take, not only to prevent this anguish and distress in your conflict with death, but also to overcome the fears of it, and so be able to meet and embrace it, is to begin a life of religion now, while you are in the morning and flower of youth. Besides a constant habitual preparation for death, which is an unspeakable privilege, you will enjoy all your days, and you will reap these special benefits by it when you come to meet the king of terrors, and to look death steadily in the face.

You will be able to reflect and look back with greater comfort upon your past life and conversation in the world than otherwise you would do, or than many other dying saints are enabled to do. You will not have so many youthful sins to come to your memory and distress you in a dying hour, as otherwise you will have. Do but consider, how is it possible that a poor prodigal that returns to God after he has consumed the biggest part of his time and talents in the service of sin and Satan, should find his account in the midst of the agonies of death, as the early convert is likely to do? Death, indeed, will eventually prove gain to every true penitent.

But then the aggravated sins of youth will afford a most melancholy prospect unto him, that has wasted away the best of his days in sin and vanity, and will, in all probability, extort such a mournful petition as that in a dying hour. *"Do not remember the sins of my youth, nor my transgressions; according to Your mercy remember me, for Your goodness' sake, O Lord"* (Ps. 25:7).

Prayer at Death

This will very much dampen the joys and comforts of his last minutes. Whereas, on the other hand, the early convert, when he comes to lie upon a death bed, may first look back and take a prospect of his past life, and then look upward, and appeal to God in the language of holy Hezekiah: *"Remember now, O Lord, I pray, how I have walked before You in truth and with a loyal heart, and have done what is good in Your sight"* (Isa. 38:3). Who but they that have had the happy experience of it can tell how great a consolation it is?

Comfort of the Holy Spirit

You will doubtless enjoy so much more of the comforts of the Holy Spirit at death by how much earlier you set out in the service of God. God will never forsake any of His children in their greatest extremity. He will afford them His enlightening, supporting, and comforting presence in their most dark and disconsolate hours. Hence that *"Unto the upright there arises light in the darkness"* (Ps. 112:4), the light of divine consolation and the joy of the Lord will refresh them in their deepest distresses.

May we therefore imagine that the early convert will miss it in his last conflict with death? Is it not much more reasonable to suppose that, since he set out early in the work of his Lord and has patiently borne the heat and the burden of the day and has now come weary to the end of his labors, that therefore his most compassionate Lord has a more refreshing cordial to revive his spirits with, now that the shadows of the evening have come upon him? See how David, one that feared the Lord from his youth, comforted himself with the hopes of this beforehand, and doubtless he experienced much more when he came to the trial than he had hitherto conceived of. *"Yea, though I walk through the valley of the shadow of death, I will fear no evil; for You are with me; Your rod and Your staff, they comfort me"* (Ps. 23:4).

The sooner you begin to live to God, the brighter your evidences for heaven are likely to be in a dying hour. You will then have this convincing proof of the sincerity and uprightness of your hearts which a later penitent will want, namely, that you renounced and abandoned your sinful lusts and pleasures for the sake of your great Savior when you were in the midst of the strongest temptations to pursue and gratify them, and during the best conditions for the enjoyment of them. Besides, it is very probable that the Holy Spirit will give a more clear and ample testimony to the truth of your graces. By this means, you will have the most ravishing prospects of happiness and glory before your eyes, and so pass through the shades of death in the chariot of praise.

An Honorable Name

Lastly, you will hereby leave a more honorable name behind you at death. The wise man assures us that the *"memory of the righteous is blessed"* (Prov. 10:7), but among these, the name of the early convert will appear in a brighter character, with fewer stains upon it and with more noble embellishments which will exceedingly recommend it to those he will leave behind. These are the distinguishing privileges and honors of early religion in a dying hour.

Now children, were these fruits you were to reap of your early conversion to God, such singular privileges alone in a dying hour would more than recompense the most diligent labors of the longest life? But I must now dismiss this second general heading and pass on more briefly to say:

Special Advantages of Early Piety

What the special advantages of early religion are like to be in the world to come. Here I will mention but these two only:

Eternal Glory

If you die young, as who knows but you may, you will certainly be admitted into the Kingdom of heaven, while the wicked and profane youth that die in their sin shall be cast down into hell. Christ will gather the lambs of His fold into His own bosom, while the seed of evil doers will be rejected and excluded forever. This will be such a distinguishing glory, that eternity itself will be short enough to declare the blessedness that will most certainly follow upon it.

Blessings in Heaven

Suppose you should live any considerable time in the world, then afterwards, you will be advanced to higher degrees of glory in the world to come. The rewards of heaven, indeed, are not of debt but of grace, as they respect us. Therefore, he that has spent the most time and done the most service for God in his day cannot, by any merit of his own, lay claim to the least degree of heavenly glory.

However, such are the sovereign determinations of divine grace, for the encouragement of early and industrious piety, that God will reward every man in the world to come, according to his works. God will render unto him not only according to the quality of his works in general, but in proportion to the quantity of them.

Parable of the Talents

This is plain from the parable of the talents that you find it recorded with the explanation in Matthew 25:10-30. It is evident that those who first begin, and do most for God in their day and generation, will be exalted to the highest degrees of glory in heaven. The chief seats in those blessed mansions above are prepared for them, and stand ready to receive them.

Therefore, as they pass out of time into eternity, they will be advanced to those thrones of glory, and from thence will they shine forever and ever, as stars of the first magnitude in the firmament of glory. What a transcendent privilege is this!

Heaven and Glory

The chief seats of honor and dignity among men are very much sought after and prized by the men of this world. Yet, the least degree of heavenly glory is infinitely more excellent than all the glory of the world put together. There is such immensity in it, that eye has not seen, nor ear heard, neither has it entered into the heart of man, to conceive of it as it really is. How surprisingly great, then, will the honor and happiness be, not only to be admitted to the glories of heaven but to be advanced to the highest degrees of that glory?

Verily, heaven itself will forever ring with the loudest acclamations of praise from those who will be the objects of this distinguishing, eternal favor.

Thus, I have passed through the various particulars at first proposed. I might have enlarged upon every one of them to very great advantage would the time have allowed.

Since it will not, I will finish the present discourse with this brief reflection upon the whole. That is, since the peculiar advantages of early religion are such as we have heard, those of you that are in your youthful days should improve the consideration of them as a most powerful argument - to seek and serve God, the God of your fathers, without any further delay. It is not possible that you should have any more alluring and persuasive motives to the duty than are contained in the thing that have already been set before you.

Having therefore nothing further to offer at this time to enforce the advice upon you, I will conclude with my earnest wish and prayer to that God, with whom is the success of all our labors, that He would be pleased graciously to bless this and all the other endeavors of this kind, which (I trust) are sincerely designed by His servants, for your highest and best good. Amen.

7

OBJECTIONS ANSWERED

Mr. Cooper, Boston, May 11, 1721

Matthew 19:22
But when the young man heard that saying, he went away sorrowful.

This is an essay to promote early piety. To teach young people that the fear of the Lord is the beginning of wisdom, that good understanding, which they who do God's commandments have, must be allowed to be very noble and worthy. In pursuit of such a design, our young people have had several discourses where they heard the duties of early piety explained, their obligations to early piety, and the advantages of early piety.

The part assigned to me towards this work is to consider the discouragements, and reply to the objections which may arise in the minds of any of them, against being religious early on, and which Satan, who to be sure, will do all he can to counter us, will not fail to cast before them.

Rich Young Persons

The text I have read and only propose to begin with, will appear, I hope, not altogether improper to the occasion, if we consider the story which it relates to. There was a hopeful, sober, and well-inclined young gentleman of a plentiful estate and in some public post, who came to Christ and addressed Him upon a most serious and important case. *"Good Teacher, what good thing shall I do that I may inherit eternal life"* (Mark 10:17). This young man was instructed in and believed the doctrine of eternal life and was concerned how he might obtain it. He was aware that something needed to be done in order to obtain it, and desired to know what it was, that he might do it. He applies himself for information about this matter, and he goes to the best - our Lord Jesus Christ, who is the great Teacher from God, who alone has the words of eternal life, and who is Himself, the Way, the Truth, and the Life. The young man employed a very fitting manner, with humility and earnestness. Mark says that he came running, and kneeled to Him, and by how he puts the question itself, he seems to be in good earnest; *"Good Master what shall I do?"*

It was a lovely sight to behold. It is truly a blessed sight to see anyone seriously concerned about their soul and another world, eagerly inquiring how they may get to heaven. It is especially a lovely sight to see young persons so concerned, so inquisitive. A lovely sight is this! But alas! How rare it is among the young people of the present day! It is too rare among young people of every quality, who are generally apt to think there is enough time for such an inquiry, but especially among those who rise up in the world in superior circumstances with respect to outward rank and estate, who, having mighty notions about this world, lightly regard the things of another, whose earthly inheritance too often takes their eyes and hearts off the heavenly.

Keeping the Commandments

Our Savior, in answer to the question of this young man, says, *"If you want to enter into life, keep the commandments"* (Matt. 19:17). There is one way of salvation for old and young, that is, the way of faith, repentance, and holy obedience. They that do not walk in the way of God's commandments are certainly out of the path of life. This is the way that God has marked out, and there is no thinking of any other. *"Blessed are those who do His commandments, that they may have the right to the tree of life, and may enter through the gates into the city"* (Rev. 22:14).

Young people are as much bound and obliged to keep the commandments of God as others are. Neither must they think that the heedlessness and inconsiderateness of youth will excuse or justify them when they wander out of the way. No, it is expected from them that they take heed to their way according to God's Word. They must bear the yoke, the yoke of God's commandments, in their youth if they would see life and obtain happiness here and hereafter. Christ says to this young man, *"If thou wilt enter into life, keep the commandments."*

The Question

The young man asks of Him again, *"Which ones"* (Matt. 19:18)? He might have concluded *"all,"* for there is the same authority prescribing one as another, and every command of God is equally obliging. But he asks, we'll suppose, for a more full and particular information, that he might know which were of the greatest importance, and which he must have a better regard unto. We should all endeavor to get as clear and distinct of a knowledge of our duty as we can. We should desire to know what is good, and what the Lord our God requires of us.

Various Commandments

Christ numbered several of the commandments of the second table to him. Jesus said, *"'You shall not murder,' 'You shall not commit adultery,' 'You shall not steal,' 'You shall not bear false witness,' 'Honor your father and your mother,' and, 'You shall love your neighbor as yourself'"* (Matt. 19:18-19). Our Savior mentioned second table duties only, not because they are of greater importance than the first, but, as Matthew Henry says, because, though first table duties have in them more of the essence of religion, second table duties have in them more of the evidence of it, and teach us that though a mere moral man comes short of being a complete Christian, yet an immoral man is certainly no true Christian. These commandments, which our Savior here mentions and recommends to the young man as necessary for him to observe and keep, have been explained to our young people in those discourses which opened the nature of early piety as it relates to others, and unto themselves.

The Reply

The young man replies, *"All these things I have kept from my youth. What do I still lack"* (Matt. 19:20)? It would have been happy for him indeed if he could have rightly and truly made such an answer as this, *"All these have I kept from my youth,"* but it was a confident boasting that revealed his great ignorance and conceit. Had he known the spirituality and extent of the divine law, that it not only forbids the outward acts, but the inward lusts and emotions of the heart, he would never have answered thus, but on the contrary, would have said with concern, shame, and grief, as the best of us have reason to do before God, *"All these have I broken from my youth."*

However, according to how he understood the law, it is thought, he spoke truthfully. Take them externally, and in the literal sense, he might have kept the commandments. He might be unreprovable with respect to them before men, though he could not be before the all-seeing, heart-searching God. He was free from any gross violation of them, and it was a happy thing that he could so speak. It is truly a favor of God to any, for which they should think of with thankfulness to Him, when their youth has not been stained by any scandalous sins. But we must not think this sufficient. We must not stop there, for mere morality will never carry anyone to heaven. It is not enough for you, young persons, that you be blameless in your outward carriage and conversation, but you must become really, inwardly, and practically religious and godly. Many cannot say for themselves what this young man did, and yet, as far as he went, he did not go far enough. He was not altogether a Christian, but was likely to come short of eternal life.

The Lack

Christ therefore, in answer to his further inquiry, *"What lack I yet?"* tells him what he must come up to if he would approve himself a Christian indeed, and so make sure of eternal life. Jesus said unto him, *"If you want to be perfect, go, sell what you have and give to the poor, and you will have treasure in heaven; and come, follow Me"* (Matt. 19:21).

Religion indispensably requires this of every one of us, that we resolutely and practically prefer heaven above earth, and portion in Christ before all the wealth and riches in this world, so as to be willing and ready to part with our all in this world for Christ and heaven if He should call upon us to. Upon no lesser terms can any of us now be the true disciples of Jesus Christ. To test this young man, therefore, and see whether he was indeed so set for heaven and eternal life as he seemed to be, Christ tries him by command: *"Go, sell what you have and give to the poor"* (Matt. 19:21) and follow Me", and take up with a treasure in heaven instead.

At this point, he went away sorrowful. He could not comply with this motion, and could not come up to these terms. He objected against this as a hard saying, and was discouraged by it from following Christ, and any longer seeking after eternal life. If religion would cost him so dearly as this, he must even be done with the thought of it. This saying of Christ was such a discouragement and objection that he could not get over. It proved to be a fatal hindrance and impediment to him.

It is now time for me to dismiss the text and context, and to apply myself to that single part assigned me in the present work, which, as I told you before, is to consider and reply to some discouragements and objections that young people may have against being religious in their youthful days.

Deprived of Pleasures

Objection I: *"If I am religious in my youthful days,"* a young person may think and say, *"I shall debar and deprive my self of those pleasures and delights of life, in which youth is the proper season for the taste and enjoyment of."*

Answer: *Religion does not wholly bar you and restrain you from the delights and pleasures of this life. Indeed, you must not make provision for the flesh, to fulfill the lusts thereof. You must not give appetite and sense its full swing. Nevertheless, there is not a total restraint laid upon you. It is not criminal for you to be cheerful and merry in conversation. Young people may use the diversions and pleasures of life that are proper to their age, as long as they keep within the bounds of innocence and moderation.*

Godliness is not as sourly illustrated a thing as you may imagine it to be. It does not give a total prohibition of earthly pleasures, but allows of, and even directs to the sober and moderate use of them. *"Go, eat your bread with joy, and drink your wine with a merry heart; for God has already accepted your works. Let your garments always be white, and let your head lack no oil. Live joyfully with the wife whom you love all the days of your vain life which He has given you under the sun, all your days of vanity; for that is your portion in life, and in the labor which you perform under the sun"* (Eccl. 9:7-9). Use this world you may, but do not abuse it. Godliness would only direct and lead you to such a use and enjoyment of earthly pleasures and delights that may be without offence to God, and hurt to yourselves.

What Pleasures Are Lost?

The pleasures which godliness requires you to deny yourselves and abandon, what are they? They are mean and base at best, suited only to the inferior part of man. They have in them more of the beast than the man, and the brute creatures may have a more exquisite sense of them than we have. What are these to a rational soul, to us, whom God has taught more than the beasts of the earth, and made wiser than the fowls of heaven? They are false and deceitful, and have in them the show of pleasure only, and not the substance, the appearance and name rather than the thing. The fruition of these pleasures does not answer the expectation.

Solomon ran a prodigious length in sensualities in the pursuit of forbidden pleasures. He tested his heart with mirth and gave himself to know madness and folly. Whatsoever his eyes desired, he kept not from them. He withheld not his heart from any joy. And what satisfaction did all this afford him? Why, truly none at all. He said of laughter *"'Madness!'; and of mirth, 'What does it accomplish'"* (Eccl. 2:2)? Again, they are vanishing and perishing. The world passes away, and so do the lusts thereof.

The pleasures of sin are but for a season, and a very short season too. They will perish in the using. They are easily disturbed and dashed, and quickly over and gone. Once more, they are destructive and deadly. Bitter sweets! They please and gratify now, but they will sting and torment hereafter. The fruit and end of them is death. *"Stolen water is sweet, and bread eaten in secret is pleasant. But he does not know that the dead are there, that her guests are in the depths of hell"* (Proverbs 9:17-18). So then, the pleasures which godliness requires you to abandon, are such as you have little reason to be fond of. However, the corrupt heart may find some reluctance in refusing them. Yet, as one aptly uses here the words of Abigail to David about his denying himself the satisfaction of being revenged on Nabal. Afterwards, *"this will be no grief to you, nor offense of heart"* (1 Sam. 25-31).

Pleasures Gained

The delights and pleasures which are to be found in the ways of godliness, are incomparably better than those which you must deny yourselves and abandon. There is this commendation given of wisdom's ways: *"Her ways are ways of pleasantness, and all her paths are peace"* (Prov. 3:17). They are not only pleasant ways, but ways of pleasantness. In the abstract, as one observes upon the place, there is such pleasantness nowhere else to be found as in these ways. The delights that are to be met with in the way of duty and religion are such as the greatest sensualist cannot boast of.

The pleasures of piety do exceed the pleasures of sin and sensuality, in the subject of them, the soul the better and more noble part, in the object of them, an infinite God, a glorious Christ, all spiritual blessings in heavenly places, and in the properties of them. They are true and solid, pure and substantial, rational and sublime, durable and lasting, not so easily dashed and broken by the little accidents and sudden changes of this life. The longer the enjoyment is, the higher the pleasure rises.

What are the poor and beggarly pleasures of this life, to the testimony of a good conscience, joy in the Holy Spirit, delight in God, and communion with Him? Those who abandon sensual pleasures for spiritual delights and holy joys, they only exchange dirt and trash for gold and pearls. Leave the garlic and onions of Egypt for the milk and honey of Canaan. O, our young people! If you did but once experience the pleasures of true piety, they would put your mouths out of taste to the pleasures of sin and sensuality. Having tasted of this new wine, you would not ask for the old because the new is better.

That pious youth, Mr. Thomas Beard, who died at about seventeen years of age, (whose life is published[1], and recommended to young people by Matthew Henry), could, from his own happy experience, write down such lines as these,

---

1. Joseph Porter, *The Holy Seed, Or, The Life of Mr. Tho. Beard.* 1711.

"There is nothing of delight in the world comparable to what I have found in the enjoyment of God. One hour's, yea one moment's communion with God, is far beyond the sensual delights of a whole life. I have met with true and solid comfort, and soul satisfying joy in the way of duty and religion." O taste and see if it be not so.

Faithfulness to God is Impossible

Objection II: *"The work of godliness is very hard and difficult, and I fear that if I try it I shall find it impossible, and not be able to go through with it."*

Answer: We would deal plainly and truly with you, and let you know the worst beforehand, so that you may sit down and count the cost before you begin to build, and may so set out as that you may not turn back discouraged by meeting with what you did not expect. We do therefore, acknowledge it to you that it is no easy thing to be a true and thorough Christian.

Those that are most acquainted with practical religion and the power of godliness, know that the Christian life is compared in Scripture to running a race, to wrestling, to fighting, all which imply difficulty, opposition, hardness, and the great need for skill, activity, strength, resolution, and patience. Godliness does not consult your carnal ease and pleasures. There are many laborious duties for you to perform, many temptations to resist, corruptions to mortify, and conflicts to endure. A few lazy wishes and faint endeavors will never carry you to heaven. You must watch and be sober, watch and pray, watch and work. You must gird up the loins of your minds, and put on and manage the whole armor of God, press on, and fight through. You must overcome the world, the flesh, and the devil, and take the Kingdom of heaven by a holy violence. Nevertheless, though the work of religion be thus hard and difficult, you should not object against it, that you may not be discouraged from it on the account hereof.

If there is any truth in religion, the difficulty that attends the practice of it cannot be allowed to be a reasonable or sufficient objection against it. If there is a God that made you, He has a right to rule you now, and to judge you hereafter. If you have immortal souls within you, that must live forever either in a world of happiness or in a world of misery, if you are hastening either to heaven or hell, and it is likely to fare with you in the other world how you have lived in this, I say, if these things are true which religion teaches, as they certainly are, and as you do believe that they are, why then, surely no pains can be judged too great to take, no difficulties too great to be undergone, for an affair of so high a concern. Can you think any effort too great to save your souls, to escape hell and obtain heaven? Oh what pains will men take, what difficulties will they go through, and what hardships will they endure in prosecuting matters of far less concern in affairs that relate only to the body and the life that now is? What trouble will men be at to get the riches, or the honors, or the pleasures of this world, travelling both sea and land for them? What a folly then, what a shame is it for you to make such an objection in this case? One would think there is nothing so difficult, but it should be readily and willingly entered upon and engaged in, if the salvation of the soul and its eternal welfare, be at all concerned in it.

Slavery of Rebellion

The difficulty that attends the practice of religion and godliness can be no sufficient objection against it. In the way of sin and wickedness, there is many times more self-denial undergone and pains taken in the service of sin and lust than the practice of religion calls for. *"The way of the unfaithful is hard"* (Prov. 13:15). *"They weary themselves to commit iniquity"* (Jer. 9:5). There is no worse slavery than to live in the pursuit of base lusts. How the sinner, in the gratification of them, is carried by violence and headlong, contrary to the dictates of his reason, and the checks of conscience! How his time is consumed there, his estate often wasted, and his body enfeebled! How many thousands die martyrs to their lusts, and are burned with as keen a fire as that the martyrs?

Sometimes, the very contrivance of sin gives sufficient uneasiness and trouble, but more especially the reflection on it. How the sinner does start and recoil at his own actions when he thinks them over!

The Troubled Sea of the Rebellious

One of the greatest troubles in this world is for a sinner to look within himself, and remember what he has done. The Scripture speaks of the condition of sinners in this world as full of uneasiness and disquiet. *"The wicked are like the troubled sea, when it cannot rest, whose waters cast up mire and dirt. 'There is no peace,' says my God, 'for the wicked'"* (Isa. 57:20-21). Such, often disguise their condition, and make an appearance of satisfaction, but God, who is acquainted with the secrets of all hearts, knows what horror rages in their breasts.

Power of Grace

Whatever difficulty attends the practice of religion and godliness, the grace of God can enable you to meet it. You are not left to struggle with the difficulties of religion in your own individual strength, but God is ready to afford you His help and assistance, who when strengthening us, we can do all things. You have not only the outward arguments of religion to encourage you to encounter the difficulties of it, but the promise of His Holy Spirit to help and assist you. *"I will put a new spirit within them, and take the stony heart out of their flesh, and give them a heart of flesh, that they may walk in My statutes and keep My judgments and do them"* (Ezek. 11:19). He is ready to do this for all that sincerely and in good earnest apply themselves to Him. Wherefore, instead of objecting against, or being discouraged from godliness, by reason of the difficulties that attend the practice of it, you should only be quickened thereby, according to the advice of the apostle, *"Let us therefore come boldly to the throne of grace, that we may obtain mercy and find grace to help in time of need"* (Heb. 4:16).

The Yoke of Christ

The greatest difficulty will be in your first setting out in the ways of religion. What in religion may seem hard at first, through the corruption of our nature, and our former accustomedness to sin, will, by the use and exercise and the grace of God, become easy. When once you are well entered in the service of God, you will find it perfect freedom. In a little time you will be able to attest to the truth that *"His commandments are not burdensome"* (1 John 5:3).

Christ's yoke, says one, grows easier and smoother. When we have born it upon us, at the very first putting on, the flesh will strive hard to fling it off. I remember to have read in the life of Mr. Philip Henry, that he, preaching from those words of Matthew 11:30, said: *"My yoke is easy,"* at last appealed to the experiences of all that had any time drawn in that yoke, and then gave his own testimony after this affecting manner. *"I,"* said he, *"will here witness for one, who through grace have in some poor measure been drawing in this yoke, now above thirty years, and I have found it an easy yoke, and like any choice too well to change."*

Sweetness and Pleasure

There is that sweetness and pleasure accompanying the practice of religion and godliness and that glorious reward following it, that far outweigh all its troubles and difficulties. I might here show, if my present limits would allow, how that in all the several acts, instances, and duties of religion, that even those that seem to be the hard lessons of christianity, there is a sweetness and pleasure to be found, not only to support but delight the soul. Her ways are ways of pleasantness, and all her paths are peace.

The Reward

What a blessed hope is set before you in the end to invite and animate you? All the difficulties of religion will be abundantly compensated by a glorious recompense of reward in the next world. Religion proposes so great a reward to you, so that if you should spend your whole life in labor and toil for it, it would be worth the while. It is the most noble goal that man's nature is capable of, set forth to us in Scripture by many chosen comparisons, as particularly by a royal throne, a glorious kingdom, and a glittering crown. *"To him who overcomes I will grant to sit with Me on My throne, as I also overcame and sat down with My Father on His throne"* (Rev. 3:21). *"I bestow upon you a kingdom, just as My Father bestowed one upon Me"* (Luke 22:29). *"Be faithful until death, and I will give you the crown of life"* (Rev. 2:10). There is nothing greater aspired after by the ambitious children of men than a crown and kingdom, and they will wade through fields and seas of blood to obtain one. Yet they strive for a corruptible crown. The crown and kingdom which Christ sets before you in the gospel are not like the crowns and kingdoms of this world: troublesome, thorny, tottering, fading things, but it is easy, steady, safe, and will never fade away. O young person, will not this so tempt and fire your ambition as to make you think all difficulty light and inconsiderable that may lie in your way? Will not this counterbalance a few days of labor and difficulty?

Trials and Tribulations

Objection III: *"But religion will expose me to many troubles and sufferings, for it is through much tribulation that we must enter into the kingdom of God, and all that will live godly in Christ Jesus must suffer persecution."*

Answer: *Troubles and sufferings are also to be met with those outside of religion. The ungodly, besides inward troubles which are the worst, are liable to the same outward afflictions that others are, such as bodily sicknesses and pains, the deaths of near relatives, disappointments, losses, and impoverishments in their outward estate. With respect to such things as these, we are told,* "All things come alike to all: One event happens to the righteous and the wicked" *(Eccl. 9:2). As to the common and ordinary afflictions of this life, you will be exposed to them outside of religion as well as in it.*

As to any extraordinary sufferings purely on the account of religion, such as the loss of liberty, estate, or life, (though indeed we should be ready to part with these in the cause and for the sake of religion, should we be called to it), you are not sure you will meet with any of these. Bonds and afflictions do not always abide the saints. God does not call every one to resist unto blood. Thanks be to God! Our lot is cast in a place and time of liberty and peace, wherein the churches have rest and are edified!

But suppose the worst, that you should be called to any such sufferings on the account of religion. Those sufferings can be but very short. The sharpest sufferings of the present time, they are *"but for a moment"* (2 Cor. 4:17). Where God calls His saints to extraordinary sufferings, He usually gives them extraordinary supports and consolations under them. Some suffering saints have said, *"For as the sufferings of Christ abound in us, so our consolation also abounds through Christ"* (2 Cor. 1:5).

A Greater Reward

Moreover, the greater your sufferings are here, the greater will be your reward in heaven. They will work out for you a far more exceeding and eternal weight of glory. *"I consider,"* says the apostle, *"that the sufferings of this present time are not worthy to be compared with the glory which shall be revealed in us"* (Rom. 8:18).

Let it be considered by you, that if you do not become godly, you expose yourselves to the endless and insupportable miseries of the next life, which the most exquisite torments of the present life are but faint resemblances of. Upon the whole of this matter, it will be your wisdom, young people, to make Moses' choice, who, when he was come to years, chose *"rather to suffer affliction with the people of God than to enjoy the passing pleasures of sin"* (Heb. 11:24-25).

Reproached

Objection IV: *"But I shall be reproached, derided and scoffed at, especially by my old acquaintance and companions, if I should become serious about religion now."*

Answer: *It is not a disgrace to be derided and mocked at, but only when one deserves to be so. The best of men have been so, such as David, Job, Jeremiah, Paul, and others of whom the world was not worthy. And I might name a greater than these, even our Lord Jesus Christ, a great part of whose sufferings were the derisions and mockings that He met with.*

The jests and scoffs you may meet with, will be so far from a disparagement to you, that they will be your honor. While they deride and mock you, others, the wiser and better sort, will esteem and reverence you, and give you their best regards.

You would better be derided by others than have your own conscience reproaching you. It does not matter in whose eyes you are condemned, if you are great in the sight of the Lord.

The reproaches by which some that sit in the seat of the scornful may reproach you for your turning into the way of godliness, will fall upon themselves, and will make to their condemnation a sorer punishment in that day, when sinners must account for all their hard speeches. But they will turn to your advantage and blessedness. Our Savior has said, *"Blessed are you when they revile and persecute you, and say all kinds of evil against you falsely for My sake. Rejoice and be exceedingly glad, for great is your reward in heaven"* (Matt. 5:11-12).

It will not be long before those who now deride and censure you will openly applaud and commend you, as the only wise and happy ones. *"We fools counted their life madness, and their end to be without honor, so how are they numbered with the children of God, and their lot among the saints?"* The reproaches you may meet with should not discourage you. Rather, they should make you more resolute in the ways of God. You should answer the scorners, as David replied to the taunt and reproach of Michal the daughter of Saul, *"It was before the Lord ... and I will be even more undignified than this"* (2 Sam. 6:21-22).

Less Prosperity

Objection V: *"Religion is no friend to prosperity. I must expect to be poor and low in the world if I become religious, for I observe that most who are religious are so."*

Answer: *It is a most foolish and absurd thing, to be influenced by external motives and temporal considerations in matters of spiritual and eternal concern. What, I beseech you, is a man profited, if he gain the whole world and lose his own soul, or what will a man give in exchange for his soul?*

It is true indeed, that the godly in the earth are often the poor of it, and brethren of low degree, but then they are in that state, in those circumstances which infinite wisdom sees best for them, and in which their spiritual and eternal welfare is most promoted and the best secured. The soul is the man. What is best for us is best for our souls. If the wicked have more of this world, they have need enough of it. For it is their portion. Deliver me, O Lord, from the men of this world, who have their portion in this life!

However, the objection is not true. Godliness is a friend to outward prosperity and is profitable to all things.

But at last, piety is the best prosperity. The merchandise of it is better than the merchandise of silver, and the gain thereof than pure gold. Her fruit is better than gold, and her revenue than choice silver.

Unfashionable

Objection VI: *"Religion is no fashionable thing as there are but few that really mind it, of any age or quality. Why should I be unique? "*

Answer: *Serious religion and strict godliness, is but an unfashionable thing in the world. Yet, it is of infinite concern to us that we heartily embrace it.*

Let none urge this objection, unless they are willing to lose the favor of God, the happiness of heaven, and their own precious and immortal souls out of gentility. Are they willing to be damned and go to hell for fashion's sake? This, I hope, you will account too awful a choice.

We should let no example influence us contrary to what is our duty and interest. We should not follow a multitude to do evil, nor be conformed to this world. The broad way is never the better for being crowded. hell will be never the pleasanter for the company that is in it.

Religion is never the worse in itself, regardless of who will, or as many as will, slight it. Sooner or later, most men testify to the wisdom of it[2]. Do you not observe, that they who care not to live the life of the righteous, yet desire to die their death, and to have their last end like theirs? Of the thousands whose deaths we have seen or heard, what one person ever recommended an irreligious life to those that stood about him, as desirable, and did not rather warn them from it as mischievous and ruinous? What one man in the world ever repented of a good life when he came to die, and did not rather, with tears for his own miscarriages, and with all the arguments imaginable exhort to it? That person, in a dying hour will wish himself no man, that has not been a good Christian.

---

2. Vid. *Dying Men's Living Words*. Published by Dr. Lloyd.

Dying You

Objection VII: *"If I am religious in my youthful days, I will die young."* This is what Satan has sometimes buzzed in the ears of some seriously disposed young persons to scare and deter them.

Answer: *Though piety does not secure a long life in this world, yet to be sure, it never shortened anyone's life in it. It is more likely to prolong it. It keeps us from those vices and excesses which shorten men's lives. Piety has the promise of long life, as mentioned in 1 Timothy 4:8: "Godliness is profitable for all things, having promise of the life that now is."*

The irreligious, to be sure, have no reason to expect to live long in the world. *"But it will not be well with the wicked; nor will he prolong his days, which are as a shadow, because he does not fear before God"* (Eccl. 8:13). We see that many ungodly ones die young. *"They die in youth, and their life ends among the perverted persons"* (Job 36:14).

To those who desire to live long in this world, the best course they can take for it is to become practically religious and godly. *"Who is the man who desires life, and loves many days, that he may see good"* (Ps. 34:12)? Solomon therefore makes use of it as an argument to persuade us to be godly. *"Hear, my son, and receive my sayings, and the years of your life will be many"* (Prov. 4:10).

Many a young convert has attained to the character of an old disciple as well as Mnason *"an early disciple"* (Acts 21:16). How many of the saints recorded in Scripture died in a good old age? We have some alive among us at this day, who can say in David's words, *"O God, You have taught me from my youth; and to this day I declare Your wondrous works. Now also when I am old and gray headed"* (Ps. 71:17-18).

Suppose you do die young, will you have a sufficient life? That promise, *"With long life I will satisfy him, and show him My salvation"* (Ps. 91:16), may be fulfilled to one who dies in youth. It is the nature of grace to wean the soul from this life, to raise it above it, and to fix it upon another. Hence, there have been found some instances of gracious young people, who have been not only willing, but have gladly desired to leave this world. He that has lived as long in this world to become fit for a better place and willing to leave this, he has lived long enough and dies full of days.

Then, if you are gracious, the days you lose on earth will be gained in heaven. There you will have length of days forever and ever.

Apostasty?

Objection VIII: *"If I begin to be religious now, it may be I will not continue so. Many have apostatized from good beginnings, and it were better never to have known the ways of God, than wickedly to depart from them."*

Answer: *The apostasy of some from good beginnings has been very sad and awful. Woe indeed to them who, having begun in the Spirit, do end in the flesh! But this should not discourage nor deter you from entering upon the ways of God. It should only serve to take you off from self-confidence, and put you upon a more humble and earnest seeking of that grace of God, which will be able to make you stand, to confirm you unto the end.*

There never was a true convert that totally apostatized. *"Being confident,"* says the apostle, *"of this very thing, that He who has begun a good work in you will complete it until the day of Jesus Christ"* (Phil. 1:6).

That proverb, *"a young saint makes an old devil,"* that is so often in the mouths of profane ones, is false and malicious. No! The young saint will more likely prove to be an angel when he is old in respect of excelling knowledge and sanctity.

The young hypocrite will prove to be an old apostate, but the serious youth, the longer he experiences godliness, the better he will like it, and the closer he will stick to it. The grace of Christ, in him and with him, will be sufficient to make him finally victorious over all difficulties, temptations, and dangers.

I Have Time

Objection IX: *"There will be enough time for me to be religious. I am young, and have many years before me."*

Answer: *This may be the most common objection, and prevails most on our young people to use it to defer and put off the great work of religion and turning to God. It normally would have required a more full and large answer to have been given to it, except that the happy labors of my reverend brethren in the previous discourses immediately preceding this, do spare me the pains. I will therefore only take the liberty to ask you who make such an objection, these two serious questions:*

1. How do you know that you will have any other time than this afforded you? Have you any lease of your lives? Have you made a covenant with death, and an agreement with hell, that you know you will stand? Is not the shortening and prolonging of your life in the hand of God, that God whom you can now so easily forget and neglect? Are you not altogether uncertain when death may be commissioned by the great God to fetch you out of this world? May you not be cut off while you profane upon hereafter? Do not you think that there are many now in the chambers of utter darkness, who presumed upon time which they never enjoyed?

I think the providence of God silences the objection at this time, when the angel of death stands with a drawn sword over the town, and threatens to come up into our windows, and enter into our palaces, to cut off the children from without, and the young men from the streets.[3]

2. How can you expect to find acceptance with God hereafter, if you neglect to seek and serve Him now? The hereafter you depend on may never come, but if it should, is God bound to accept you then? Must He take you up with the refuse and dregs of your time, when you served the world, the flesh, and the devil, with your flower and prime? May He not then justly say, *"Go to the gods you have chosen and served?"*

We would not discourage the repentance and endeavors of sinners who have come to the end of their time. The mercy of God in Christ may prevent a total despair then, but verily it is, as one calls it, an extraordinary act of sovereign divine grace when those are accepted.

Oh then! Do not run all hazardous with respect to your souls and another world, as you will do if you hearken to that suggestion. But, resolve, by the help of God that you will not defer setting about the work of serious religion any longer. Do not think of a more convenient season. Today, while it is called today, harden not your hearts. Be as speedy and instant as he was, *"I thought about my ways, and turned my feet to Your testimonies. I made haste, and did not delay to keep Your commandments"* (Ps. 119:59-60).

---

3. Preached at a time when the smallpox had spread through the town, a distemper which (though frequent in other places) is the terror of us in New England. Scarce a quarter part of the town (it is thought) have had it, and none of the youth under nineteen or eighteen years of age. It has since spread into many families.

Many Ways to God

Objection X: *"Even if I had a mind to be religious, there are so many different paths in religion, that I should be at a loss which to take. Some cry this way, others that, so that I know not which to choose and fall in with."*

Answer: *I am afraid that those who object after this manner only pretend the differences in religion to excuse their declining that which really they hate, for they are only the lesser matters wherein Christians differ, and it is unreasonable, on the account of these to forsake those great and necessary things, wherein all are agreed.*

We are not aiming, in our present design, to bring you over to the interests of a party. No, the piety which we principally press on our young people is what all true Christians own to be necessary. What all good men, though of different persuasions on lesser accounts, are united in. What all people, when they come to die, advise and commend and bear their testimonies to.

The use you should make then of these differences in religion, is not to throw off all religion, but to be inquisitive after truth. For this end, you should diligently study the word of God, and humbly seek His Spirit to lead and guide you. I will add too, that you should not be reluctant to consult and advise with the faithful ministers of God. *"For the lips of a priest should keep knowledge, and people should seek the law from his mouth; for he is the messenger of the Lord of hosts"* (Mal. 2:7). All your ministers would be glad to afford you what light, direction, and help they can. I am sure you should not neglect them, to take counsel and receive light from those who may not be as able to give it to you, nor to have the same concern for you, and that aim only to bring you over to their own party and interest.

As to what way of worship and form of administration you should attend, I will only say this unto you: choose that which, after humble study and prayer, you seriously and conscientiously judge to come nearest to the Holy Scriptures, the only rule and standard of faith and practice, the most likely to promote the power of practical godliness in your lives, and the salvation of your precious souls in the end.

Thus, I have made some reply to the most considerable objections which many of you may make against being godly in your youthful days.

Obstacles in the Way

Consider now, dear young people, of what has been said, and may the Lord give you understanding in all things! The Lord help you over all the blocks and bars that lie in your way, and, by His special grace, effectually determine your thoughts and hearts for Himself and service, and bring you into a serious and delightful walk in the ways of piety! May you be so wise, as early to choose the good part, which cannot be taken away, and may you afterwards be agreeable to your early choice! May you be able to say in the end, with the psalmist, *"I have chosen the way of truth; your judgments I have laid before me. I cling to Your testimonies"* (Ps. 119:30-31).

EXHORTATIONS & DIRECTIONS to YOUNG PEOPLE

Mr. Foxcroft, Boston, May 18, 1721

2 Timothy 2:22
Flee also youthful lusts; but pursue righteousness, faith, love, peace with those who call on the Lord out of a pure heart.

We are still on the excellent theme of early piety. In the course of this lecture, you have already had the nature of early piety defined, and the various parts distinctly illustrated, the obligations stated, the advantages represented, and the many objections obviated. The business now allotted me, as the conclusion of the whole matter, is to make some application or improvement of the foregoing discourses, in a use of exhortation and direction. Though indeed in them, there may have been offered something of this tendency, yet if we consider the vast weight, as well as reach of the argument, together with the remaining cold and careless unconcern about it, visible in too many of our young people, it will sufficiently appear that the task assigned me is not an excess or superfluous addition.

As to the passage of Holy Scripture now read, I will not stay in showing the connection, nor in opening the contents of it. It may suffice to say, we have here an address to a young man and an exhortation to early piety. I have chosen the words only as an agreeable foundation or decent introduction to that part of the subject which falls to me, and the prosecution of it I will now immediately apply myself to.

The method I propose to go in is this: I will speak to the secure and thoughtless sinners among our young people next to the thinking and awakened then to the penitent and regenerate.

Secure and Insensible

The first sort of young people to be exhorted are the habitually secure and insensible. Too many, I am afraid, are of this unhappy character among our young people, as well as elders, despite the repeated solemn calls, warnings, and exhortatations they have had from time to time. Therefore, there is need to address the secure. O that we might succeed in these our last attempts!

Let every unconcerned and unconvinced young person now, before the Lord, consider that I am particularly speaking to him, in the name of God. God who searches the hearts, who expects you take heed how you hear, and will one day call you to an account, in His great and dreadful name, I am now speaking to you. O consider this, young people, and dare not to turn away your ear, nor harden your heart, but hearken to the voice of God and see that you refuse not Him that speaks from heaven.

Hearken to the counsel which is brought you, and send us not back to our master with that melancholy complaint, *"Who has believed our report"* (Isa. 53:1)?

Let me entreat you to suffer the exhortation. Be persuaded then, oh sinner, to strike off carnal security, and seek after religious convictions. Awake, awake, O sinner! Awake, you sluggard! Rise from your bed of sloth. How long will you slumber? Will you not think and stir yourself? O sinner, open your eyes to behold the light, open your ear to discipline. Rise out of the dust, shake yourself, and no longer fold your hands to sleep. Do this now, my brother, and deliver yourself. Give not sleep to your eyes, nor slumber to your eyelids. Escape for your life, escape to the mountain, lest you be consumed. Deliver yourself as a deer from the hand of the hunter, and as a bird from the snare of the fowler. Go to the ant, you sluggard, consider her ways, and be wise. Awake, you who sleep, and arise from the dead. Knowing the time, that now it is high time to awake out of sleep, therefore, cast off the works of darkness.

But, as the prophet speaks, *"To whom shall I speak and give warning, that they may hear? Indeed their ear is uncircumcised, and they cannot give heed. Behold, the word of the Lord is a reproach to them; they have no delight in it"* (Jer. 6:11)! Indeed, when I consider how powerful an orator Satan is, and how great is the deceitfulness of sin and the infatuation of self-love, I am almost tempted, in despair of success, to desist from the present attempt to awaken the secure and to break off in the words of the same prophet, *"I am full of the fury of the Lord. I am weary of holding it in. I will pour it out on the children outside, and on the assembly of young men together"* (Jer. 6:11)

But when I consider again the wisdom and the power of Christ (whose ambassadors we are, and on whose blessing we have leave to depend for prosperity in our sincere endeavors), my hopes revive, and I cannot but reassume and proceed in His name and strength to press the exhortation. O! That He, who can make dry bones live, would now breathe in His Word, and speak to the heart and conscience of every one, while the Word is sounding in your ears.

Arguments to Persuade

What arguments and expressions shall I choose? O, that I might be direct to such, as will affect and penetrate deep! God is our witness, whom we serve in the gospel of His Son, that our hearts' desire and prayer for you all is that you may be saved. Now therefore, as though God did beseech you by us, we urge you in

Christ's stead, be reconciled to God, and as workers together with Him, we beseech you, that you receive not the gospel of God in vain. By all the compassion you owe to your perishing souls, we beg you, yea we command and exhort you by our Lord Jesus Christ, that you now, even now without any further delay, examine yourselves and let such considerations as these which follow, be of weight with you, to hasten your seeking after sound convictions. I will endeavor only to hint at things, a few things; and leave you to enlarge on them in your retired meditations, because otherwise I foresee I will be tedious.

Consider the great sinfulness of your present security. Great is your wickedness herein. Your guilt is very obvious and prodigious. Your carnal security implies the blackest ingratitude, the basest disingenuity, the vilest injustice, rebellion, and presumption. It betrays a secret infidelity, and proceeds from accursed principles. It is a manifest disobedience of the perceptive will of God. It is a slighting of the threatenings of His law, a condemning the promises of His gospel, and an opposing of the gracious designs of His Word and ordinances and providences.

It is a high contempt cast on the blessed God. It is a dishonorable reflection on His wisdom and love in Christ. It is a reproach of His justice, holiness, and truth. It is a defiance of His infinite power, an abuse of His mercy, and a mocking of His patience! It is an insolent spurning at His favor, a neglecting of His service, and a wasting of the time and talents He has given you, and a preferring the Devil over Him. Furthermore, it denies the Lord that bought you, and tramples under foot the Son of God. It also resists the Holy Spirit, and spites the Spirit of grace.

Your security then, is a heinous iniquity, and unspeakably aggravates it and immovably hastens upon you the guilt of all your other sins. O secure young person, labor to see what horrible guilt lies upon you! Let the past time suffice to have been spent in this dreadful wickedness. Now wake to righteousness, and sin not.

Consider the absolute inexcusableness of your sinful security. You have no plea in the world to cover your guilt. Your security is willful and chosen. It is against many calls and cautions, both in the word and providence of God. You cannot therefore, plead that you have not been duly warned and called. God and men are witnesses to this. You cannot plead invincible ignorance of the way of salvation, the necessity of conversion, the need of convictions, and the methods in order to it, for light has come into the world, and you choose darkness.

You cannot plead impossible difficulties in the way, for grace is offered, grace sufficient, and you refuse it. You cannot pretend lack of encouragement, for great and precious promises are set before you. You cannot pretend lack of helps to assist you, for you have all necessary means of conviction and awakening. You cannot have the face to pretend lack of leisure, that you have no time to attend the necessary care of your soul, being engaged in other matters of higher importance. There is nothing of an equal or comparable moment with that, or, being as a servant in a continual hurry of care and employment and not free, for you may redeem time from your bed and table and otherwise.

Know you have a master in heaven whose service must not be dispensed with on any score whatever. You cannot be so absurd as to pretend any unfitness of the present time, or say that you are too young to concern yourself about the grave matters of religion, for that which is at all times your indispensable duty, and so necessary to your present (as well as future) safety and comfort, cannot be begun too soon. Besides, how many others, no fitter by nature nor riper in years than you, have early sought and rightly improved their convictions, to their saving repentance?

How Will You Answer?

What then will you say when God will arise? How will you answer it, O young person, when God will bring you into judgment, that you have not remembered your Creator in the days of your youth, but have walked in the ways of your own heart, and in the sight of your eyes? Verily, you have no cloak for your sin. Every mouth will be stopped. Behold, heaven, earth, and hell will bear record against you, even your own conscience will speak as a thousand witnesses, and strike you into silence and confusion. Whoever remains graceless in the day of grace will be found speechless in the day of judgment.

Consider the extreme folly of your present security and the madness of continuing in it. O, how unreasonable is it! It is a prodigy of madness, as well as wickedness. He is unworthy the name of a man, that allows himself in it. O, that you could see what a drunken, stupid, blind, and mad thing it is! I have not words or thoughts big enough to reach the height of this folly. Your carnal security and ease is most irrational and absurd in its nature, grounds, and motives. It is an open contradiction to all genuine principles of reason, an offering of violence to all the laws of prudence, and the dictates of normal self-love. He might well be called a fool, who said to himself, *"Soul, take thine ease."* Let me here offer a few hints, to illustrate this point a little.

Presumption

Your security is unreasonable, in that it is without all ground or stands on a deceitful bottom. It is chiefly owing to careless inadvertence, or wild presumption, or wicked infidelity. Your present ease and quiet is altogether false and delusive. It is mere forgery and fiction, a lying vanity, and empty show of peace. It is as different from a true solid rest of soul, as a killing lethargy from the sweet and refreshing sleep of health, and at best, it is but for a moment. O, the stupidity then of your beloved dreams!

Folly

But your folly will be more glaring if we consider what a miserable state it is you are secure and easy in. Your misery is great upon you. The miseries of your present state are dreadful and astonishing. You are at a distance from the blessed God, and are under His wrath and curse, in your person and enjoyments and all the work of your hands. You are at war with God, in an active as well as passive sense. The carnal mind in you is at enmity against God. And you are at war with yourselves. Innumerable hurtful lusts are in you, which war against the soul and with one another.

Bondage

You are under the vilest servitude and bondage, possessed by the Devil, chained down to the earth, and sold under sin. You are also in a state of the utmost poverty and indigence. It is the character of secure Laodicea and belongs to you. *"You are wretched, miserable, poor, blind, and naked"* (Rev. 3:17). You have no interest in God as your portion, in Christ as your Redeemer, in the Holy Spirit as your Comforter.

You are without grace, mercy, and peace at present, and without any right to glory and happiness hereafter. You are altogether unable to deliver yourself out of this deplorable condition, and are also unwilling to accept deliverances.

Stupidity

O, what amazing stupidity and indolence this is! What a riddle is here? Senseless and quiet under such a pressing load of evils! Hear O heavens, and be astonished O earth; surely you are more foolish than the beast that has no understanding and has not the knowledge of a man! To languish away in an insensible life in such a miserable state! Nothing more unreasonable! Nothing so unaccountable!

Danger

There are innumerable dangers that threaten you, which are as awful as the miseries are sorrowful, and call for the most awakened resentment and horror. Oh what a dark and dreadful prospect is there for you, secure sinner! God has threatened to punish the men that are at ease from their youth and settled on their lease. You are daily liable to, and may well expect, outward and temporal judgments, which may soon end or much embitter your life, for the whole creation is armed against you. Though through infinite divine patience you may prosper in your wickedness, yet this will be only for a moment and you will soon find yourself in judgment.

But you are especially in danger of spiritual miseries. Your security exposes you to all manner of snares and temptations to the most gross and criminal sins, and even invites our subtle enemy to take advantage hereby to pursue his malicious designs to your eternal ruin. Moreover, you are in danger of neglecting the means of grace, at least the saving benefit of them. Even if you voluntarily and studiously remain secure, you are in danger of being finally abandoned by God, judicially hardened, and growing worse and worse under the means of goodness. Scripture affords us an abundance of sad examples of this.

Eternal Miseries

Finally, remember that you are in hourly danger of eternal miseries. Beyond and after all the former evils, there are unknown plagues in reserve for unregenerate sinners in the coming world, which you are every moment in the utmost hazard of. If you die unconvinced and impenitent, you will immediately be punished with an everlasting destruction from the presence of the Lord. And die you will shortly. You may die in youth, you may die speedily, perhaps suddenly, without warning and without relief. You have abundant reason to fear lest this be your dreadful portion, for it is what the word of God threatens to rebellious obstinate sinners.

"He who is often rebuked, and hardens his neck, will suddenly be destroyed, and that without remedy" (Prov. 29:1). The providence of God always presents us with awful executions of this threatening upon others, and you may reasonably expect the same treatment from vindictive justice. It is a wonder of infinite patience that you have been spared hitherto, but how much longer will divine compassion reprieve you, is an uncertainty of trembling consideration. If you should be snatched away unexpectedly and hurled down suddenly into the horrible pit and devouring fire, how will the sad surprise, amazingly aggravate your fearful doom?

Consider the Hazards

Now reflect on these things, O secure sinner! Think of the awful hazards you incur, and see your egregious folly. Surely madness is in your heart! Were you not blinded by the god of this world and under the power of strong delusions, I think it could not be that you should thus despise your own soul and expose yourself to such dreadful risks. How mad would it be for a man to sleep carelessly on the top of a mast or the brink of precipice! Much more is it in you to indulge your guilty slumbers over the flames of hell and under the loud thunders of heaven. It is folly in the exaltation thus, to sleep in the midst of so many and such dangers. Surely such deserve the character of drunken children, and you may well lie down in your shame and confusion cover you when you think of your astonishing stupidity and temerity, which declares you more foolish than the filthiest worm, that by a natural instinct, studies self-preservation.

Exercise Prudence

Remember, it is a point of prudence to consider future events, to view things in their last result as well as present aspect. Hence the wise man observes, *"A prudent man foresees evil and hides himself, but the simple pass on and are punished"* (Prov. 22:3). It is the folly and ruin of many young people that they are so easily deceived with present appearances and will not look forward to the end of things, will not realize future dangers and govern themselves by the serious thoughts of invisible realities.

Present Opportunity

Remember, it is a point of prudence to improve the first convenient season for the accomplishing affairs of weight and necessity, and not to forego a present opportunity on the presumption of another or better hereafter. But now, how contrary to this principle is the conduct of secure sinners? It is certain, repentance is a matter of absolute necessity which must be seasonably minded, or you are undone forever. You are sure of no season but the present. And yet how do you let slip one opportunity after another? You will sleep securely today and defer till tomorrow, though you cannot promise yourselves to live until then. Oh, what distraction is it thus to depend on a remote possibility, and venture your everlasting concerns on so great an uncertainty!

Best Opportunity

Remember, it is a point of prudence to choose the fittest seasons. As to the work of repentance, the time of youth, the present time, is the best opportunity for it. By an early conversion, the great ends of repentance are most promoted, which are the glory of God and our own peace and welfare. This thought should animate you to early seek after conviction which is a necessary to conversion. The reasons that should move you to seek convictions at all, have the same force, now as ever to engage you, nay are more obliging now in the days of your youth.

In the time of youth, convictions are to be attained with greater ease. Youth is the age of discipline, tractableness, and tenderness. Now, as a youth, natural conscience is most awake and sensible and strivings of the spirit ordinarily most effectual. Now, you are clogged with fewer impediments, and so convictions will have easier admission.

Change Is Easier

Besides, at this age, your convictions will be lighter and more easily borne. If repentance is delayed, you will not be brought to it without more pains and groans, and more tears and terrors. The longer you sleep in carnal security, the opening of your eyes will grow more difficult, and the scene more terrible. More of hell must be flashed in your face, and there will be more amazing aggravations of sin to rack the conscience and rend the heart. Consequently, greater horrors will take hold of you.

The stings of sin will be more in number and greater in pain, the wounds of spirit deeper and the workings of conscience more violent afterwards than in youth. Delays will not mollify the anguish, but will double the torment of painful convictions. It is wretched folly then to let go the present season. It is contrary to right reason which teaches us the wisdom of prevention, and forbids our doing that which will lay a foundation for later sorrow and regret.

How great then is your madness, O sinner, in that by your present security in the day of youth, you are making work for a bitter repentance hereafter, and taking an unhappy method to render your conversion more dolorous and difficult, if you do at length obtain mercy.

Again, if convictions are quickly begun and entertained, the work will sooner be over. Ordinarily, young converts are not under preparatory terrors as long as others. As the agonies of the new birth in such are more tolerable, they are more transient, and such have fewer *"after pains."*

Vain Dream

These things abundantly show that the time of youth is the special season for repentance. Do not then put repentance off on the vain dream of a more convenient opportunity hereafter. Behold, now is the day of salvation. Be wise therefore, and improve the present day for the seeking convictions. Perhaps this may be your only opportunity, but supposing it be not yet, surely it is the best. The present season is attended with peculiar advantages, and there are no objections occurring now, but what will equally lie against a future season when it becomes present, nay, will then be much enhanced and more invincibly embarrass you. Every moment's continuance in sin puts you farther off from convictions, and is a closer approach towards incurable obstinacy. Finally, remember, if you perish at last, your destruction will be of yourself. You choose death and invade damnation. You will be justly charged with self-murder. Is not this the height of madness?

Thus, young people and brethren, I have shown you in some little measure, how foolish your present security is, and how extravagantly mad it will be to persist. O, that you could be brought to see and realize these things, and see how your conduct interferes with all rules of sober reason.

Foolish, Drunk, and Stupid

Reverence the character you sustain of rational creatures, and think it beneath the dignity of your nature to be so foolish, drunk, and stupid, as before. Young people are very apt to indulge a sinful self-conceit and wicked pride. More of us perish by this lust than by any other, and here, we must study mortification.

But there is a commendable self-conceit and lawful pride which would be well if we had more of it in us. I mean a proper sense of our real excellency as reasonable beings, a just value for the noble powers we are endowed with, and an ambition to do things worthily, and a holy scorn and aversion to all that looks like or leads to sin and folly as degrading our nature, and laying our honor in the dust. O, let such a principle be cherished in us. Let us be too proud to liken ourselves to unclean devils by sin, or liken ourselves to untaught brutes by stupidity.

Vain Bravery

Not a few there are indeed, who take a pride in carnal security, and vainly boast of a resolved bravery, as wise and heroic in them. Tell them of such and such a thing that they have been warned about, they turn it off with a smile and brag that for their parts they never heed, they mind not what is said to them, never thought on it since, and so glory in their shame. These fools in Israel have instruction and despise wisdom. But do not do so, you, my brethren! The wisdom of the prudent is to understand his way and to look well to his goings, and happy is the man that fears always, but he that hardens his heart, will fall into mischief, and at his end will be a fool.

Hearken unto me therefore, O ye children! Hear instruction, and be wise, and refuse it not. To such among you as are now a little apprehensive of the guilt and folly of your security, and begin to inquire how you may obtain spiritual convictions and get out of your secure state?

To such I would offer a few words by way of counsel and direction. Here in the first place, let me caution you to be aware of all the cases of security, and impediments of awakening. Watch against everything that tends to nourish sloth and to prevent your desiring, or obtaining convictions. You must learn the causes of security and not be ignorant of the devices of Satan. You must watch and guard against them.

Vain Ignorance

Take heed then, of affected ignorance, for it is the ruin of many. They shut their eyes against the light that shines about them, or turn away their face, whereby their foolish heart is darkened and Satan keeps his goods in peace. Beware of false reasonings and prejudices. Shut your ears against all the cavils and objections of an evil heart of unbelief, which is enmity against God and is not subject to His law. Take heed you do not entertain wrong and abusive apprehensions concerning God, as being full of revenge, which will tend to dampen all thoughts of a reconciliation. Conversely, do not think of God as being so full grace and pity that He cannot be disposed to damn His own creatures, however sinful, which will tend to harden you from the fear of God.

Beware of misconceptions concerning Christ, as if His satisfaction had taken away the obligation of the moral law as a rule, removed the necessity of repentance and personal obedience, and purchased an order for wickedness. Beware of light thoughts of sin, as it not being so evil and offensive to God. Take heed of loose thoughts about the Scriptures compared to their divine original as just translation. Beware you do not disbelieve or make light of unseen eternal realities.

Depraved Senses

Don't listen to your depraved senses to be judges between things present and things to come. Hearken not to their false reports, and flattering promises about worldly objects. Beware of an immoderate esteem of the world, lest this engross your thoughts and cares, desires and joys, and fatally divert you from minding your everlasting concerns, as was the case of the unhappy young man (Matt. 19:16-22). Also, abandon evil company. Forsake the foolish, and live. Break off from your drunken clubs or merry meetings, and leave the company in which you are likely to have your rioting, your whoring and wantonness, and evil deeds of darkness. Depart, I pray you, from the tents of these wicked vain persons, and touch nothing of theirs lest you be consumed. Follow not their vicious practices, nor listen to their bad advice.

Conceited Self-Righteousness

Further, beware of deceiving yourself with a comparative righteousness. Young people are very apt to take the measure of their own worth on religious accounts (as well as others) from those who are inferior to them and to swell in their own conceit when they behold others more profane and wicked than themselves. They trust in themselves that they are righteous, and despise others. They are pure in their own eyes, if they are just a little more refined than the looser rabble. Therefore, they are secure and easy, and with the vainglorious Pharisee say, *"God, I thank You that I am not like other men"* (Luke 18:11). O, take heed that you do not depend on a mere comparative righteousness.

Passing Privileges

Finally, let the children of the kingdom, the posterity of godly parents, beware of trusting in the privileges of their birth and education. Do not presume on your knowledge of God or your natural relation to the friends of God. Do not depend on your baptism. This alone profits nothing. Do not rest in your parents' prayers for you. Value them, but do not overrate them. All the interest they have in heaven will not purchase salvation for you! If you repent not, you must perish even as others, who are the seed of the wicked and aliens from the commonwealth of Israel.

Verily, though Noah, Daniel and Job (and Abraham and Moses with them) were your ancestors and advocates, yet they should deliver neither son nor daughter that abides impenitent. If you sin against the Lord, the hope of your fathers, think not to escape the vengeance, which awaits the children of disobedience, nay, a most heavy vengeance, aggravated by the advantages you enjoy, which are many and great. Beware then, of trusting in your pious parentage and the privileges of it. Receive these cautions, O secure sinner, and improve them.

Furthermore, let me now advise you more directly in the following particulars. Endeavor to furnish yourself with knowledge in spiritual things. If you would awake to righteousness, you must get the knowledge of God as is intimated in 1 Corinthians 15:34. Without knowledge the heart cannot be good. Illumination is a necessary precursor to conviction, though conviction be not a necessary result. Alas, many professing believers, even preachers of the gospel, are really slaves of Satan, yet none can become the true servants of God without Christian knowledge. You must learn to know your own selves, what you were, conceived in sin, what you are since, apostate, and what you are still capable of being. You must seek the clearest apprehensions of God, absolutely and relatively considered, and of Christ the Redeemer, the Holy Spirit, the great Teacher, Sanctifier, and Comforter. You must understand the terms of salvation. You must know the rule of duty, together with the grounds and reasons of it. You must get acquainted with the divine threatenings and promises.

Knowledge

If you are not duly informed of these things, no wonder that you are secure and impenitent. If then, you would obtain effectual convictions, before all gettings, get understanding and search for knowledge, as for hidden treasures. Labor after a teachable frame of spirit. Use the means and cry to the God of knowledge for instruction. Thus, you are exhorted and encouraged to do (read Proverbs 2-8 at your leisure).

Persuade yourself to meditate. Commune with your own heart seriously and often about the solemn truths tending to conviction. Simple speculation without practical reflection can never have any warm and sensible effects on your hard heart. Barren knowledge only puffs up the fleshy mind. It is musing that makes the fire burn. David said: *"I thought about my ways, and turned my feet to Your testimonies"* (Ps. 119:59). The prodigal son's repentance began here.

"But when he came to himself, he said, 'How many of my father's hired servants have bread enough and to spare, and I perish with hunger! I will arise and go to my father'" (Luke 15:17-18). It is the lack of serious consideration that ruins multitudes. *"But Israel does not know, My people do not consider ... they have forsaken the Lord"* (Isa. 1:3-4). If men would but examine themselves, it may be they would repent (1 Kings 8:47). What is the reason, that in time of sickness or imminent hazard, conscience recovers some sense, sinners are more concerned than at other times, and fearfulness surprises the hypocrite? It is because now they are considerate. They look about them, and take a fuller view of things, and are therefore more affected. As faith is necessary to make spiritual things evident, so is consideration to make them efficacious. This gives divine truths weight and warmth, and applies them with power to the soul and is the leading step towards conversion. Let young people be persuaded then, to give themselves to meditation. Learn to fix your thoughts and contract a habit of thinking - sober, serious thinking. With the reason that becomes men, and the solicitude that becomes sinners, set yourselves to meditate on divine and spiritual things, especially those truths which most tend to awaken you to repentance.

Consider Sin and Purity

O, think on the guilt, pollution, and misery of your natural state. Think on the evil of sin in its nature and consequences. Think on the sins of your past lives. Consider them in their quality, number, and aggravating circumstances. Think on the infallible knowledge, infinite purity, inflexible truth, almighty power, and exact righteousness of God, whom you have provoked by your sins. Think on the reasonableness and perfection of His precepts, the dreadfulness of the threatenings, and the greatness of the promises thereunto.

Think on your absolute inability to fulfill the law, to expiate your sin, or to endure the curse. Think on the blessed provision made for you in Jesus Christ. Think on the greatness of the salvation purchased by Christ and proposed in the gospel, the freeness and grace of the offer and the condescension of the terms and the assistance tendered you. Think how much it cost the Son of God, even His own most precious blood, to procure this redemption for you. Think often of Christ and Him crucified, of Christ and Him glorified.

Think particularly on the agonies of His soul, which was exceedingly sorrowful even unto death, under a sense of sin and apprehension of the wrath of God, and endeavor, after some initiation of Him, to meditate on the vanity and meanness of all earthly things. Think on the certainty and awfulness of approaching death, judgment, and eternity. Think on the glories and joys of heaven, the miseries and pains of hell, and the infinite folly you are guilty of in not taking a timely care to secure the former and avoid the latter.

These are some of the things, which you should meditate upon, and a due consideration of them would have a rational tendency to impress your hard heart and awaken you out of your sleepy insensibility.

O sinner, I beseech you then, think on these things sadly, in the fear of God. Set your heart unto all these things, give yourself wholly to them. Let your meditations be voluntary and chosen, free, and unconstrained. Let them also be leisurely, frequent, and solemn. Take time and take pains, and be diligent in the work.

This is a duty of vast importance and therefore, must not be trifled in, much less neglected. This also is what you have a natural capacity for. You can thus meditate if you will. You do not lack ability, nor do you lack opportunity. This is the best use of your thinking powers. Your thoughts are generally busy, and to what can you employ them that is of greater weight or value than the subjects before mentioned? Your minds are very apt indeed to run upon your worldly affairs, pleasures, profits, honors, and friends. But alas! How foolish are you in this, since those other meditations recommended above are incomparably more necessary, excellent, delightful, and beneficial, and are in themselves are no greater toil and labor.

Excuses

What excuse then, can you frame? What pretence to palliate your neglect of holy spiritual meditation? Verily you are inexcusable, O man, whoever you are, that lived in the omission of them. Be exhorted then, to dismiss your vain thoughts with shame and regret for them, to overcome your natural aversion to spiritual meditation, and speedily set about this great work.

Debate with Your Heart

O that I could persuade you this night to retire and spend a little moment in serious debates with your own heart on the sin and folly of present delays in the affairs of your soul! Henceforward, accustom yourself, now and then, to separate some small portion of your time in solemn consideration of some awakening truths. Possibly, this might be blessed to your saving conviction. I think this would be a necassary thing to do for your soul. There can be no rational expectation of your thorough awakening, until you can be brought to sober thinking. But, if I could persuade you to this, and you would engage in it in earnest, it would be a hopeful omen of your conversion.

O therefore deny not this much to yourself. Deny it not to God, if you will deny it me. I have told the truth: *"Consider what I say, and may the Lord give you understanding in all things"* (2 Tim. 2:7). If you force me to conclude in harsher terms, they will be still the oracles of God. *"Now consider this, you who forget God, lest I tear you in pieces and there be none to deliver"* (Ps. 50:22).

You must, with great industry and care, improve all proper outward helps and means to improve spiritual conviction.

With a view to this end, diligently read the Holy Scriptures, and other pious books. Do not misspend your time and endanger your soul by conversing with idle, lewd, and profane authors, which tend only to exalt folly and alienate you more from the life of God. But read religious authors, books of devotion, practical sermons, and books regarding pious lives, particularly such as are most suited to the care of the secure. Choose with caution. Read with deliberation and diligence.

More importantly, be conversant with the blessed Bible. Give yourself to reading in the law of the Lord, which is *"perfect, converting the soul ... making wise the simple"* (Ps. 19:7). Read your Bible frequently. Look into it day and night with a teachable and obedient spirit, with attentive consideration, with firm belief, and a wise application of what you read to your own soul, by way of trial and of charge. Observe these directions in reading your Bible, and this will probably be a successful means of your awakening. The apostle tells Timothy, who, from childhood had known the Holy Scriptures, *"which are able to make you wise for salvation through faith which is in Christ Jesus. All Scripture is given by inspiration of God, and is profitable for doctrine, for reproof, for correction, for instruction in righteousness"* (2 Tim. 3:15-16).

Attend the public ministry of the Word. The preaching of the Word is an effectual means of convincing and converting sinners. The truth of this doctrine has been, through the riches of divine grace, confirmed in innumerable instances. Attend then on the Word preached.

Look on the public ministry as a divine institution. Realize the special preference of God with His faithful ministers. Let every one so account of them as of the ambassadors of Christ, and stewards of the mysteries of God, and when they speak according to the law and to the testimony, receive their message not as the word of man, but as the Word of God.

Choose Preaching Carefully

Let me here advise you to be careful (though not too careful) in the choice of the ministry that you commit yourself to the conduct of it. Beware of an ignorant ministry, a ministry that is merely speculative, or one that is superficial, and at best only throws a few squibs at grosser sins, but seldom (if ever) touches on more hidden spiritual sins, nor attempts to lay open the misery, guilt, and danger of a natural state, and show sinners their need of Christ for righteousness and strength.

Choose not a ministry of either of these perilous characters. But fix yourself under a skillful and orthodox, a godly and experienced and a practical scriptural and searching ministry, which preaches Jesus Christ and shuns not to declare the whole counsel of God, and studies to commend itself to every man's conscience in the sight of God.

Be Quick to Hear

Having chosen well, also improve well. Be swift to hear, and take heed how and whom you hear. Attend with constancy, reverence, and diligence, as a humble learner. Lay aside all superfluity of naughtiness, and receive with meekness the engrafted Word, which is able to save your soul. Receive the truth in the love of it, mix the Word with faith, hide it in your heart, and labor to press it on conscience, both in the hearing and afterwards.

Under the conduct of these rules, make use of the Word preached as instrumental for conviction and repentance, and it may be that it will work effectually in you, as it did in those of whom we read in 1 Thessalonians 2:13.

Be aware of how God is awakening you. Thus, are you under afflictions yourself? Labor to get your heart suitably affected. Do not set God's judgments at defiance, nor harden yourself against discipline. Solomon sometimes observes that the rod gives wisdom. If they are bound in fetters and be held in cords of affliction, then He shows them their work and their transgressions that they have exceeded. He opens also their ear unto discipline and commands that they return from iniquity.

Afflictions by a natural efficacy tend to soften and humble. When God's hand is upon you then, take this opportunity to press after convictions. In the day of adversity, consider the rod, and who has appointed it. Receive correction, set in with providence, and work together with God. Thus, Manasseh and the prodigal son improved their outward afflictions to their inward humiliation and repentance.

Let me add here, observe and study to affect yourself with the death of other young people and the sad outcries of the impenitent in their last moments. Look on what befalls others, as a warning and call from heaven to you, and let it strike an awe upon you. Let the sudden deaths which you have seen or heard of at any time alarm your fears and rouse you out of your security. When it is a time of spreading mortality, when death rides in triumph in our streets, this is a loud summons to everyone, especially to young people who are most exposed to infectious diseases, a loud call. This is to cause us to turn unto Him that smites. We should wisely observe, repent, and improve such dispensations, and study to affect our hearts, that we may tremble at the arm of the Lord stretched out, and humble ourselves under His mighty hand. This, God expects (see Joel 2:1).

Walk and talk with the wise. *"He who walks with wise men will be wise, but the companion of fools will be destroyed"* (Prov. 13:20). *"The fruit of the righteous is a tree of life, and he who wins souls is wise"* (Prov. 11:30). I have before directed you to desert the unnecessary company of vain persons. I now further advise you to take yourself to the society of the awakened and converted, whose pious example and discourse, serious counsels and reproofs, may be blessed by God for your conviction.

The apostle speaks of some who do not obey the Word, as if they might be won by the good conversation of their associates. Some have been wrought upon, this way whom the Word never did reach. Resolve then, to be a companion of those who fear the Lord. Acquaint yourself early with the godly, and perhaps their holy communion may be a savior of life unto you. As live coals kindle those that are dead, so to converse with lively saints may have a warm and enlivening influence upon you. Light may break in upon you, as a flame from a sparkling fire! These are the external helps, which you are advised to use.

Be sensitive to the whispers of your conscience. Observe and cultivate the least beginnings of conviction. Hoist and spread the sails when the wind begins to blow. Open all the powers of your soul to the divine breathings, and cherish the faintest impulses of the Holy Spirit. In the use of means, wait and watch for convictions. Embrace them at their first offer or approach. When light flashes in upon you, do not let your heart rise in opposition, or your mind divert and start away. But whatsoever good thought is at any time shot into you, immediately close with it and fasten it, as a nail in a sure place. Whatsoever devout affection begins to stir in you, do not go to stifle and smother them, but carefully nourish them. Back the first motions of the Spirit with close consideration and agreeable prayers, by which method a little spark may happily kindle into a living flame, and a small ray of light prove the dawning of the perfect day.

Seek God by prayer, for convictions. Prayer indeed should precede, accompany, and follow the use of means and endeavors, and it is an excellent means itself. Pray to God then, for pardon and other mercies, for conviction and repentance, which are the gift of God. Beg God that He would send His Holy Spirit to convince you of sin, of righteousness, and of judgment. Realize that God only is able, to effectually enlighten and awaken you, and in the belief of this, to cease not day and night crying to God, that He would open your eyes and turn you from darkness to light.

Beg that He would not suffer you any longer to trample on conscience, to resist the Spirit and be content in your bondage. Beg that He would not leave you to your own foolish heart and trifling endeavors in seeking after convictions. Beg that God would shake you out of your false peace and security, inspire you with a just concern for your perishing soul, and that He would give you seeing eyes, hearing ears and a contrite heart.

But if you expect to obtain the desired blessing, you must be diligent and constant in seeking it. Accustom yourself to transient, spontaneous prayer on all proper occasions, which will wonderfully tend to fix your thoughts and warm your heart and perhaps may be the means of lasting impressions. Keep up a stated course of more solemn prayer, and in the name of Christ, importunately beg for the teaching and convincing influences of the Divine Spirit. Look to your own spirit, and watch over your senses when calling upon the Lord. Do not hurry over your prayers and hasten to rise from your knees. Make a solemn business of this duty.

A Secret Place

Retire into some secret place, and devote some time to the performance of it. Content not yourself with broken petitions, put up when in company with others, or in your bed. Nay, but *"you, when you pray, go into your room, and when you have shut your door, pray to your Father who is in the secret place"* (Matt. 6:6). Make a conscious effort of doing this morning and evening at least, and endeavor to be fervent in spirit, and continue as an infant in prayer without ceasing. Cold formality and remissness in prayer drive away the Holy Spirit. I believe there is not a more common and fatal impediment to conversion than the neglect of, or negligence in closet duties. Beware of them.

Thus, I have given you some imperfect advice, what methods to take in order to cultivate conviction. O secure sinner, we charge you before God and the Lord Jesus Christ and the elect angels, that you observe these things. But know, if you will not hear all these words which I testify unto you this day are on record, and will rise up in judgment against you, God forbid!

A Message to Those Who Are Awakened

It is time now to hasten to the second branch of the exhortation. Having spoken to the secure, I am now to address those among our young people who are under some convictions and awakenings. I hope there are not a few who are inquiring the way to Zion, with their faces turned there. Unto you I will therefore now offer something by way of counsel of direction. The Lord, who knows who they are, make it a word in season to them that are weary!

Give Thanks

In the first place, let me exhort you to be thankful to God for your present troubles and convictions. See the hand of God in them. Look on your present trouble of conscience as the work of the Spirit, whether common or special. They are God's terrors, His arrows. They must not be imputed to Satan, to yourselves, or to distemper of body, as the original cause. No, for it is the hand of God, which thus writes bitter things against you, and makes you to possess the iniquities of your youth. Own and adore God here. Also, see the mercy of God unto you. Prize your convictions and be thankful. Do not resent your trouble as a misery and unhappiness. It is ten thousand times more eligible than carnal security, which is the broad road to hell.

Consider that this trouble of conscience is the method of the Divine Spirit with all that are brought home to God, though there are very different degrees of it. He humbles before He exalts. Moreover, this seems requisite in the reason of things, as a necessary preparation to saving faith. For Christ will not be precious to any, until sin and wrath become bitter and burdensome to conscience. Then hereby, you are brought near the kingdom of God and may take encouragement from the invitations of the gospel, which are peculiarly directed to such as labor and are heavy laden.

Your present trouble is a symptom of intended mercy. It is a wholesome discipline you are under. It is the Spirit of God that is wounding you, and you need not fear a lance in the hand of love and tenderness. O, do not regret your case then, but be thankful to God that you are not left to such a spirit of slumber, as many others about you are, and as you also deservedly might have been. Do not envy the secure their quiet and ease, which is false and groundless, and makes them the objects of scorn and pity, rather than of envy.

Be careful to preserve your present convictions and watch against all that threatens you with the loss of them. You are in great danger, for the Devil hates to see you under this trouble. He is afraid of losing a subject and gnashes his teeth in vexation. Be sure he will use all his art and strength to recover and secure you in his own possession. He will make use of the world without and a deceitful wicked heart within to accomplish his malicious designs upon you. The flesh, world, and the Devil are in a cursed concert to rob you of your present convictions, or defeat the end of them. This speaks your danger, and loudly calls upon you to watch and pray that you enter not into such temptations that may endanger you.

See then that you do not espouse any flattering and stupefying principles. There are a vast variety, agreeable to the tendencies of corrupt nature and the dictates of the carnal mind, which sinners, in their distress, often eagerly imbibe. Then you will be lulled into security and drowned in perdition. Watch against all such opinions.

Take Care in Listening

Be careful therefore, what books you read. Beware also what teachers you consult in your troubles. There are many spiritual swindlers as well as natural ones, ones that poison sick souls, as others do sick bodies. From such, withdraw yourself.

But, do not decline a faithful searching ministry, because you cannot fit under it with a quiet easy conscience, as the apostle has foretold some would do (2 Tim. 4:3-4). Neither dare to hide or deride the convictions of the Spirit, as is the manner of some, nor treat them as unwelcome guests, by flying from them, or resisting of them. Again, beware of procrastination. Do not elude conscience by idle excuses. Take heed you do not betray your soul into ruin by pretended resolutions of future repentance. Take heed you do not abuse the doctrine of the spiritual impotence of human nature, and of the difficulty of repentance and obedience, and make them a pretence for sloth and present delay.

Take heed you do not presume on the patience of God, and because you are young, put far from you the evil day, and, apprehending no present danger, be tempted to leave your conversion as a matter of future concern and suffer good dispositions to wear off and die away from time to time. Again, have a care of proud self-sufficiency and of undue confidence in the means of grace, without a proper respect to the Lord, whereby you will dishonor and affront the Holy Spirit and provoke Him to suspend His divine influences, where the most promising means and best endeavors will be insignificant, and you will necessarily return to former security.

Rash Resolutions

Beware of making rash resolutions in your own strength, whereby you will forfeit the aids of divine grace and provoke God to justly punish your pride and presumption. Again, take heed of indulging any secret lust, or persisting in any known way of wickedness, which will offend the Holy Spirit, and will defile and cloud and harden conscience.

Self-Righteousness

Again, beware of a self-righteous spirit. Take heed of valuing your own tears in the place of Christ's blood, of advancing your own performances into the place of His meritorious obedience, and setting your own prayers in the room of His intercession.

If you indulge such a legal Pharisaical spirit, you may, perhaps, pacify conscience hereby, but you will only inflame the wrath of God yet more against you and provoke the Spirit to leave you.

Discouragement

Beware of discouragement, as you must not give way to false hopes, so neither to despondencies. Do not take up any desperate conclusions, as if there was no hope nor help for you. This will check and chill convictions, weaken and obstruct the motions of the Spirit, and tempt you to abandon yourself to sullen melancholy or drunken security.

Worldly Engagement

Finally, beware of all worldly enticements and entanglements. Endeavor to get above the frowns and flatteries of the world. Take heed lest you fall asleep on the soft pillow of external ease, pomp, and pleasure. Be blind to the deceitful smiles and deaf to the tempting charms of a vain world. Take heed, lest the cares of this life choke the Word, and you lose your convictions in a throng of worldly fears, projects, and employments. Multitudes do drown in the sea, or bury in the earth, or barter away in the shop, or let one care or other suppress and shift off the convictions they receive in the house of God. Unhappy business has slain its ten thousands. Take heed lest being careful and encumbered about many things, you forget and forfeit the one thing needful.

Evil Company

Furthermore, beware of evil company. This was cautioned against before as tending to keep sinners secure. Indeed, those under conviction have as much need of being warned against this temptation, as those in security. For how often do vain companions persuade the convinced sinner off of serious resolutions, and laugh him out of a pensive frame, or tease away his troubles? O, save yourself therefore from this untoward generation. Have no fellowship with the unfruitful works of darkness. Resolve with the psalmist and say, *"Depart from me, you evildoers, for I will keep the commandments of my God"* (Ps. 119:115)!

Also, beware of being infected by evil examples. The security of others is, no doubt, a common temptation to young people. They see their companions, and most important, too often their elders, their parents, or masters and mistresses, these they observe are light and vain, and this prompts them to shake off awakening thoughts and fears. Beware, O young person, of this all too common snare. Let neither fear nor love of any betray you into an imitation of their security. Dare to be singular in that which is good. Do not give way to a vicious shame or false modesty, which may tempt you to sinful compliances with others.

Carnal Friends

Furthermore, beware of carnal counsels in the day of your distress. Unbelieving friends are some of the worst counselors in this case. The best advice that such miserable comforters ordinarily give is to heave off troublesome impressions, to enjoy oneself and friends, and the comforts of life. What numbers of young people have fatally miscarried under hopeful convictions by hearkening to such unhappy advice?

O, stop your ears against the baneful counsels of carnal acquaintance. Consult not with flesh and blood. *"My son, if sinners entice you, do not consent"* (Prov. 1:10). Listen not to the ungodly whispers or clamors of men of corrupt minds, however you may be related to or dependent on them. In a word, harden yourself against the mocking and scoffing of those who are at ease in Zion. Put on courage and resolution, for want of conscience is not seldom over awed and born down against its own light and bent.

The Wiles of Satan

Thus, I have cautioned you against some of the many wiles whereby Satan diverts or perverts convictions begun in young people. O, study the various policies of the enemy. Be not ignorant of his devices, lest he get an advantage against you. Learn where his strength lies, where your weakness are, the Delilah's lap you are in danger of sleeping in, and be upon your guard. Be jealous over yourself, and fear lest there be some hidden temptation which, through your ignorance or carelessness, may secretly undermine and evacuate your present convictions and so perhaps work your ruin.

Consider the Judge

Consider how your great Judge keeps an exact memorandum of all the motions of His Spirit and your entertainment of them, and will one day call you to an account for them. How will you answer it if you quench your convictions? If you do thus, verily your guilt and your folly will be great. This will be to add rebellion to sin. Hereby, you will fight against God, disobey His voice, abuse His patience, and affront His Holy Spirit. You will impiously and basely fly in the face of your great physician and despise the only remedy. You will hereby provoke the grieved Spirit to forsake you, which is a judgment not a few of the risen youth of this degenerate day are under, and you will highly gratify the unclean spirit, and invite his return into his old dwelling with more strength and company than ever, and so your last state will be worse than the first, more miserable and more dangerous. You will then be in danger of growing worse and worse, and treasuring up wrath against the day of wrath. You will be in danger of sudden destruction, and greater damnation.

If you reject or lose present convictions, you will be laying up for yourselves dreadful remorse and horror, and will pay dearly for your folly in the days of your serious reflection, if ever you are converted. Let these considerations deter every awakened sinner from a relapse into security and everything that tends to, or borders upon it. Whatever you do, keep conscience awake beforehand. Quench not the Spirit by neglect or any undue methods. Now that He is making a visit of conviction to your conscience, be tenderly careful, lest by any ill treatment or a lack of suitable entertainment, you cause Him to leave you, or become displeased and grieved.

Labor to promote the vigor and genuine efficacy of your convictions. Endeavor by all means to cherish and quicken every good motion. Lay yourself open to the convictions of the Spirit, and let them have a free and full operation in you. Do not be content, that they should stagnate, much less languish and decline. Do not think to limit the Holy One, either as to the measure or duration of your troubles. Take heed that you do not deceive yourself with only a seeming and partial work of conviction.

See that your convictions are true and sound, from right principles and motives, and endeavor to fasten and perfect them every day, that they may rise into a clearer light and stronger flame, 'till the sun of righteousness shines upon you with healing under His wings, and the day dawns in your heart. Endeavor to get forward into the work of humiliation and contrition, else your convictions will be of no real benefit to you. Rest not till you have arrived into a state of evangelical repentance. This brings me to the last thing under this heading.

Labor after a true and thorough conversion to God. Rest not in your present state, but seek after the washing of regeneration and the renewing of the Holy Spirit. Do not stop at convictions and imperfect beginnings of repentance, but labor after an unfeigned closeness with Christ, and complete conversion to God.

Peter's advice to those who were pricked in their heart was, *"Repent, and let every one of you be baptized in the name of Jesus Christ for the remission of sins"* (Acts 2:38). Paul's advice to the trembling jailer was, *"Believe on the Lord Jesus Christ"* (Acts 16:31). Be exhorted then to return to God in the way of repentance and hasten to Christ in the way of faith. Otherwise, you can never find rest for your troubled soul. All the weary steps you have already taken toward your salvation will be lost labor. You are not far from the Kingdom of God, and will you suffer yourself to perish on the very borders of Canaan? To go to hell by the gates of heaven, as the foolish virgins did is dreadful indeed, and how bitter will be the reflection? You are in danger of this through the temptations of Satan and the treachery of an evil heart that is ready to side with him.

Be exhorted then to work out your salvation with fear and trembling. Strive to enter in at the straight gate, for many will seek to enter in and will not.

Make Haste

What you do, do quickly. It is a matter of life and death, and requires haste. No advantage is to be gotten by delays. A great deal of good is lost hereby. Your troubles are needlessly prolonged, and many evils incurred. Besides, you do forfeit the grace of God, without which you cannot improve your convictions to effectual repentance. Behold, now is the accepted time. Yet, for a little while is the light with you. Walk while you have the light, lest darkness come upon you. Now believe in the light, that you may be the children of light.

True Conversion

Let no man deceive himself. Beware of mistaking the nature or the signs of conversion. Remember, conversion does not lie in nor is evidenced by a visible profession and form of godliness, a reformed life and moral virtue, inward legal terrors and transient qualms of religious melancholy, some volatile sparklings of devout affection, some sudden starts of desire or flashes of joy, a dead faith and presumptuous reliance on the merits of Christ, or a seeming peace and serenity of mind, after great terrors of conscience and an apprehended work of conviction.

There are too many who deceive themselves with these things, judging their state good, either upon wrong principles, or false evidences. *"There is a generation that is pure in its own eyes, yet is not washed from its filthiness"* (Prov. 30:12). But the day is coming when the Searcher of hearts (who cannot be deceived and who will not be mocked) will judge the world in righteousness. Be jealous then, over your own heart, that you do not deceive yourself with a partial or superficial work of the Spirit, instead of a true and thorough operation. Be careful that you do not mistake the true character of the regenerate, that you do not content yourself away with anything short of them, neither rashly apply them.

Use all proper means conducive to conversion. Attend on the ordinances of God, especially the Word preached, which is the ordinary vehicle of sanctifying influences. Study the gospel. Meditate much on the promises of God, whereby awakened sinners are made partakers of the divine nature, and on the blood of Christ, which is the only way to purge your conscience from dead works to serve the living God. Discover your case and go for counsel to some tender, faithful, judicious, experienced Christians, and particularly the ministers of the gospel, whose business as well as delight it is to show you the way of salvation and assist you under your spiritual troubles.

See that you use these and all other means dependently, with an eye to Christ as the head of influences, without whom the best means will be ineffectual. Use them diligently. Use all appointed means, public and private. Improve all proper opportunities, and spare no pains. Let heart and hand be engaged and make a work on it. Content not yourself with lazy wishes, or cold attempts, which is the next reason of many sinners failing of the grace of God (Prov. 21:25).

Yet, do not rest in the bare use of means or think you can obtain the desired end by your own solitary endeavors. Open your case to God in prayer. Carry your complaint to the throne of grace and beg for converting influences from above. Have all your expectation from God in and through Christ. Pray in the name of Christ, plead His merits, His power, and gracious promises. Plead earnestly and pray humbly, for *"God resists the proud, but gives grace to the humble"* (James 4:6).

Unworthiness

Acknowledge your own utter unworthiness. Adore the sovereignty of divine grace and submit to the methods of divine wisdom. Be content that God should take His own way in bringing you home to Himself, though it be through great terrors and sorrows. Be willing to wait on His time. Resolve humbly to take no denial and give Him no rest. Though there be long delays, yet wait patiently for the Lord, supporting your hopes by that word of promise: *"The one who comes to Me I will by no means cast out"* (John 6:37). All that ever obtained mercy, sought it on this encouragement, *"It may be that the Lord God of hosts will be gracious"* (Amos 5:15). Go also and seek the Lord while He may be found. Ask, seek, and knock, with unceasing hope and unfainting importunity. Thus *"Draw near to God and He will draw near to you"* (James 4:8), *"and will send forth "justice to victory"* (Matt. 12:20).

Finally, having thus sought God for help, now take another step. Test whether quickening and regenerating influences are not commanded from above for you. Remember how, when Christ directed the man with a withered arm to stretch forth his hand, he immediately attempted and was enabled to do it. Now imitate this great action. In the belief and hope of divine assistance, try to lift up your soul and stir up yourself to lay hold on God and do the acts of a soul returning to the Lord. Get up and be doing. Set yourself in the strength of Christ to go through the whole process of active conversion. Give not sleep to your eyes until you have endeavored this, and do not stop trying until you find the symptoms of a thorough work of repentance toward God and of faith towards our Lord Jesus Christ wrought in you.

So I have finished my address to the awakened youth. And now, the good Lord keep this in the imagination of the thoughts of your heart and prepare your heart unto Him! I hope I leave some of you inspired with never-dying resolutions to be waiting on the Lord in the methods now directed to.

Those Who Fear God

The third and last branch of the exhortation is to the regenerate, the converts of Zion. Some are there among our young people, as bad as the times are, yea many through the grace of God do we behold walking in the truth. I hope I speak to not a few such at this time. Now, you that fear God, give audience. Take the exhortation to heart, which speaks to you as unto children.

Be counseled to endeavor after a well-grounded hope and assurance of your good estate.

I begin with this advice because to me, it seems to lie in the foundation of such other counsels, as are given to the regenerate. *"Therefore, brethren, be even more diligent to make your call and election sure"* (2 Pet. 1:10). Rest not in uncertainties, but labor after the assurance of faith. To this end, study your own hearts and be much in self-examination. Try yourselves by just rules and be deliberate, prudent, impartial, prayerful and frequent in this work. Cease not until you come to a rational satisfaction about your regenerate state, which will be a mighty incentive to duty, enabling you to take the comfort that belongs to you, and will be a great support and defense in hours of temptation. For want of that, many lose the comfort and neglect some of the duties of early piety, which is sad.

Study thankfulness to God, the greatest thankfulness. Give God the glory of your conversion. Beware of ascribing too much to means, instruments, and endeavors. *"He who glories, let him glory in the Lord"* (1 Cor. 1:31). See His efficacy and adore His wisdom, power, and grace, which have abounded toward you. Let your heart and mouth be filled with admiring praises.

To excite your gratitude and wonder, often look back on your natural condition and take a view of the guilts, miseries, and dangers of it. Consider also the superlative excellency of the work wrought upon you, and the blessedness of the state you are brought into, a state of justification, adoption, and sanctification, and of habitual preparedness for a glorious eternity.

Consider the special and unnumbered advantages of an early conversion, and what a far more exceedingly glorious prospect it affords you. Consider how God has made you to be different from innumerable others. Remember also what provocations you gave the Holy Spirit to forsake you. These reflections require your thankful admirations. Wherefore, say, *"I thank You, Father, Lord of heaven and earth, that You have hidden these things from the wise and prudent and have revealed them to babes. Even so, Father, for so it seemed good in Your sight"* (Matt. 11:25-26).

Keep up a very humble frame of spirit. Remembering what humiliations you passed through in conversion, and considering what you are at present, still at a distance from God, still dependent on free mercy for all you need, still a sinful creature, doing little for God, often rebelling against Him, and in all things coming short of His glory, still feeble and impotent, and understanding that without His special help, you will become an easy prey to every temptation.

Understand that you are still in danger of such apostasies that may blemish your name, gall your conscience, and cause God to hide His face. O, remember these things and let them check all the tendencies of a corrupt heart to spiritual pride. Be not high minded, but fear. I think to add here, do not proudly murmur if you do not presently obtain those joys you looked for. If you meet with temptations and troubles within and without, do not repine. You are not now dealt with unjustly. Nay, all is in love to you. God is now training you up to live a life of faith. Perhaps He is, by His present methods, ripening you for great consolation, or preparing you for great usefulness hereafter. Beware then of every murmuring, and of every self-exalting thought.

Bring forth fruits of repentance and walk in newness of life. *"As you therefore have received Christ Jesus the Lord, so walk in Him"* (Col. 2:6). Put on the livery of

Christ and take upon you the badges of christianity. Make an open profession, order your conversation aright, and show forth the praises of Him who has called you out of darkness. *"For you were once darkness, but now you are light in the Lord. Walk as children of light"* (Eph. 5:8). Flee youthful lusts and live soberly, righteously, and godly.

See that you walk circumspectly. Walk by rule, the gospel-rule. Study it, govern yourselves according to it in the whole work of obedience, as to matter and manner, principles, motives, and seasons. The Scriptures were written to give the young man knowledge and discretion. Young people are directed to cleanse their way by *"taking heed"* of it according to God's word (Ps. 119:9).

Therefore, keep the rule always before you, and exercise yourselves always to keep your consciences void of offence. It was David's resolution in his early days, *"I will behave wisely in a perfect way"* (Ps. 101:2), and it should be yours. Youth is apt to be heady, venturous, and inadvertent, which often betrays into sad mistakes and miscarriages. But be not you so. Be wary and vigilant. Reverence conscience, consult much with it, and be sensitive to all its genuine directions. Look well to your goings. Look about you, and take example from the wise, caution from the foolish, and take heed lest you fall.

Be ever sensible of dangers. Keep up a jealous watch over your hearts and a strict guard over your senses, appetites, and passions. Keep yourselves from your own iniquity. Suppress the first motions of lust. Flee the very occasions of sin, as the goodly Hebrew youth thus secured his integrity. Remember young Dinah's folly and fall, and do not needlessly run into the way of temptations. Be careful with whom you contract close relations. Take heed how you dispose yourselves in apprenticeship, and in marriage.

Be careful in the choice of a calling. Let it be one that has fewest spiritual snares and will afford you most advantages for your souls. Study to order your affairs with discretion, so as not to hurt your grand interests. Be careful in choosing your place of abode; endeavor to settle where you may have the best opportunities and accommodations for promoting the glory of God and your own spiritual good.

Be watchful over yourselves in all conditions. Some of you are born to riches and honor, others to want and commonness. Let the poor and afflicted among you watch against discontent at the disposals of divine wisdom and goodness and against envying at the prosperity of others. Begin while you are young to learn the art of contentment and this will have a happy influence upon you all your days. Those who are prosperous, live in ease, and make a figure in the world, let such be thankful, humble, self-denying, heavenly-minded, and fruitful in every good work, and thus you will be prepared for whatever changes there may be in the right hand of the Most High.

Again, be circumspect in all matters of lawful liberty, in which case young people especially are very apt to offend, and as hard to be convinced and reclaimed. Take heed then to yourselves in all things, that you act agreeably to the laws of charity, by the rules of decency and of expediency, under the restraints of Christian sobriety, and with a just deference to the wise counsels and cautions of parents and superiors. See to it that your diversions are well-principled and well-regulated. Let them be as those that are of good report among us. Let them be seasonably entered on and timely broken off, moderately pursued and well intended, to fit you the better for serving God and your generation, which should be your primary delight and satisfaction.

Choosing Friends

Furthermore, be very circumspect as to your company and conversation. Be careful in choosing your associates. Do not degrade yourselves with Nebuchadnezzar to herd with the beasts. Let a vile person be condemned in your eyes, but honor them that fear the Lord, and like David, be a companion of those who keep the commandments of God, who are most likely to be friends to your souls, whose fruit is a tree of life. You may visit wicked persons, as their physicians, but not as their companions, lest you catch infection from them. Take such for your associates, as may be assistants to you in the affairs of your souls, and for a special friend I would advise young people to choose one that is of more experience than themselves and so capable to direct them. One that is somewhat more advanced in age and rank, whose presence may carry some awe with it, and whose admonitions may be of more weight.

As you should be circumspect in choosing your acquaintances, so likewise in using their society. Be wise and wary in your visits, that these be not a fruitless waste of time. In your occasional conversation, at all times, endeavor wisely to introduce and keep up profitable discourse. In your talk of secular affairs, let your language be such as may show a godly simplicity, and show that the spirit of this world has not the ascendant over you. This is to walk in wisdom.

But, if in conversation, your study is to please men by appearing worldly wise or facetious and entertaining instead of seeking to approve yourselves to God by being grave, pious and edifying, certainly now you walk not circumspectly, but as fools. Let young professors then be exhorted to make their acquaintance and converse together as spiritual and profitable as may be.

Living With Others

Here I might add, let such young people that live in the same house or neighborhood, by mutual agreement, oblige themselves to special watch and care over each other. Speak often one to another. Comfort yourselves together, and edify one another, even as you also do. Watch over each other in brotherly love. Be faithful monitors, every one to his brother, and let every one be ready to hearken to friendly counsels and reproofs. When the righteous smite you, let it be a kindness, and let the wounds of a friend be as excellent oil.

Dangers

Thus, I have shown young people in several instances how they are to walk circumspectly. And O, that you would all be persuaded to endeavor to walk in that way. In order to do this, consider how you are obliged by your profession and engagement thus to walk. Consider also what dangers and difficulties attend the Christian life, arising from inward corruption and outward oppositions which call for the exactest care and greatest watchfulness.

You are setting out in a world full of states and in an uncommon day of temptation. Without the greatest circumspection, you will be in imminent hazard of such falls into sin, as will wound your conscience, disturb its peace, and defile its purity.

Moreover, consider that you are under the most critical inspection. The jealous eye of an all-seeing God is upon you continually, who will be highly provoked if you are secure and negligent, which should awe you, I think, into the strictest watch over your hearts and ways, that you may walk before Him unto all well-pleasing.

Again, the eyes of men are upon you. Good people have their eye upon you. Their desire is toward you, their delight is in you, and their expectations from you are great. This should, by a principle of ambition, lead you to be careful in your walk.

Furthermore, wicked people look on you with an evil eye. These watch for your halting, they will be glad to see you careless, and they wish for your falling. Seeing you fall would rejoice (as well as harden) them exceedingly. Again, the devils keep an envious eye over you. They observe you narrowly. They are continually longing and laboring to ensnare you. If you are secure and heedless, you expose yourselves to their subtle devices, and if you fall by them, they will triumph over you, insult, and vex you.

The Encouragement You Have

Consider the many encouragements you have to be walking circumspectly. You have an unerring rule to lead you. You have, to animate you, the example of our Lord Jesus Christ, and of many saints who were holy and wise in behavior from their youth, and you have all needful assistance tendered you and the promise of great rewards, which will, by vast excesses, more than counterbalance and compensate for all the cares and pains of a circumspect walk.

In a word, this Christian vigilance and prudence is the strength and beauty of the soul. Therefore, keep your heart with all diligence, that none take away your crown. *"Watch and pray, lest you enter into temptation"* (Matt. 26:41). *"He who trusts in his own heart is a fool, but whoever walks wisely will be delivered"* (Prov. 28:26).

Let young people study to adorn the doctrine of God your Savior in all things, and to walk worthy of the holy vocation wherewith you are called. You are the children of the day, and we exhort every one of you, that you would walk worthy of God who has called you unto His kingdom and glory, and order your conversation as to the gospel of Christ. Let your light shine before men, and study to be real and visible ornaments to your profession.

For this end, guard against all evil affectations, that your good be not evil spoken of. Put away all childish vanities and endeavor to be manly and discrete in your whole deportment. Abstain from all appearance of youthful lusts, that the word of God be not blasphemed. Endeavor to be exemplary in all those things, which are acceptable to God and approved by men as lovely, venerable and praiseworthy. Abound and excel in all instances of piety and devotion. Show a profound veneration of all that is sacred. Be strict in observing the Sabbath. Show a very reverent regard to the Holy Scriptures and to the ministers of Christ as stewards of the mysteries of God. Speak with awe of God and holy things, and exhibit the utmost gravity in the worship of God, a visible alacrity in His service and a well-ordered zeal for His glory. Be of a generous spirit as to the disputable points and lesser circumstances of religion.

Further, endeavor to excel in all social virtues and relative duties. Distinguish yourselves for eminent justice and uprightness in your dealings. Show gratitude to benefactors, brotherly kindness, charity to the poor, peaceableness, forbearance, a forgiving spirit, patience under injuries and affronts, meekness under reproofs, mildness in disputes, tractableness and submission to the advice of superiors, dutifulness to parents, obedience to masters, fidelity to all trusts, modesty in apparel, and wise in speech. Again, study to excel in all more solitary virtues: self-denial, aloofness from the world, mortification of sensual pleasures, frugality, temperance in sleep and diet, chastity, purity, reservedness, and application to good business and industry. You should endeavor to exceed and outshine others in these moral qualifications and deportments, as well as in the instances of more vital and essential piety.

Early Usefulness

Finally, begin early to study usefulness. Aim at being public blessings in your day. Young converts are the seed and hope of the next generation, as old disciples are the defense and delight of the present. Therefore, begin early to get fit for your master's use. Get furnished for and ready to perform every good work. Cherish a public spirit in yourselves early and what little services you are capable of in your respective spheres now in the days of your youth. Shine as lights in the family, in the school or college, in the church, and in the commonwealth. Shine as bright as you can in your various spheres, and study to be diffusive blessings. Particularly endeavor to promote the conversion of other young people of your acquaintance, and take all proper methods to cultivate good beginnings in one another, according to the advice before given.

In these and other ways, young people should study to honor the gospel and adorn their profession. This you should be led to from considering how the gospel has been the means of advancing you to great happiness and dignity, from a view to the glory of God, which will be abundantly promoted by such carriage, and also from a regard to your own credit and interest, whose consideration should inspire you with heroic resolutions. Furthermore, this is what the Word of God expressly enjoins as the duty of young people, particularly in the second chapter of the epistle to Titus, which excellent portion of Scripture you will do well to consult very frequently.

Let young saints endeavor to grow in grace. Furthermore, we beseech you young people and brethren, and exhort you by the Lord Jesus, that as you have received of us how you ought to walk and to please God, so you should abound more and more. Do not rest in any present attainments, but study to make progress in virtue and all goodness. Diligent tradesmen at their first setting up have their minds intent upon improving their stock. Here, let not the children of this world be wiser than you. Let not the truth of grace content you, but aspire after a gradual rise. It was the apostle's exhortation to young Timothy, *"You therefore, my son, be strong in the grace that is in Christ Jesus"* (2 Tim. 2:1-2). *"Flee also youthful lusts; but pursue righteousness, faith, love, and peace"* (2 Tim. 2:22). There must be a patient continuance in well doing and studious endeavors to perfect holiness in the fear of God.

Growth

Growth in pure and practical religion is the chief blessing on this side of the heavenly places. We are to grow in conformity to Christ, who has left us a perfect example of early piety. This is to be changed into the image of God from glory to glory. This is the way to grow in the favor of God and in the comforts of the Holy Spirit, in usefulness to the world, in ripeness for heaven, assurance of salvation, and a capacity for more exalted degrees of future bliss and glory. Surely then, the thriving Christian is the wisest, the most blessed, the richest, and the happiest creature out of paradise. To flourish and increase in holiness is infinitely preferable to the highest advances in the wealth, wisdom, and honor among men of this world.

Fruit

That is what God demands and expects from you. He looks for much fruit and, O, how pleasing to Him will be the fair and rising young trees, spreading out and hanging full of early ripe fruits! Moreover, that is what you are under the strictest engagements to study, and have special advantages to pursue. Now in the days of your youth, you have fewer hindrances, greater opportunities, and perhaps you have a long time of growth before you. O, improve your singular advantages, and fail not the Lord of His righteous expectations.

How shameful will it be for you to be outgrown by later plantings than yourselves? How ignominious to be outstripped in the Christian race by others that set out after you? This will be the event perhaps, if you are idle or trifling presently. You will defeat one great design of your early conversion, by slack and sluggish endeavors in youth. O therefore, follow holiness now with active zeal, cheerful vigor, and resolute perseverance. Covet to excel, and strive to outrun, to outdo, and outshine others. This is a laudable emulation, a happy contention, which God will crown with approbation and success. O, begin early to aim at and reach after an eminent proficiency in godliness.

Humble Sense of Need

For this end, maintain a humble sense of your need of further sanctification, and mourn under the relics of corruption in you. Be much in the exercise of grace. Repeated acts corroborate the habit. It is perhaps a day of small things with you at present, but if you are diligent and constant in the exercising of grace, you will make gradual improvements toward perfection. Be faithful in a little. *"For to everyone who has, more will be given, and he will have abundance"*

(Matt. 25:29).

Industriously use all proper means. Observe all the ordinances of God with a view to and a desire to grow in grace. As *"newborn babes, desire the pure milk of the word, that you may grow thereby"* (1 Pet. 2:2). Carefully attend the Lord's Supper, which is a means, admirably effective of increasing in grace, but that is too much neglected in these unhappy times of apostasy. Be frequent in devout meditation, and solemn self-examination. Learn to do all common actions after a godly sort. Have your conversation much in heaven, by often contemplating on it, and by making it the main scope and design of your actions. Keep the holy example of Christ ever in your eye. Be also followers of them, who through faith and patience inherit the promises. Frequently renew your holy resolutions.

Dependence

Finally, be much in prayer and the exercise of faith, which purifies the heart. Live dependently on God in Christ. In the humble sense of your own wants and weakness, have all your reliance on the Father of lights and seek Him through Jesus Christ for all needful aids and recruits of grace continually. The life you now live in the flesh, let it be by the faith in the Son of God, in whom it has pleased the Father that all fullness should dwell. Trust in Him for confirming and quickening influences, and for a blessing on ordinances and providences, that all may work together for your spiritual good. *"But those who wait on the Lord shall renew their strength; they shall mount up with wings like eagles"* (Isa. 40:31). They shall grow as the lily and cast forth their roots as Lebanon, and their leaf shall not wither.

Now our Lord Jesus Christ Himself, and God, even our Father who has loved us, and has given us everlasting consolation and good hope through grace, comfort your hearts and establish you in every good word and work. We pray to God that your whole spirit and soul and body be preserved blameless unto the coming of our Lord Jesus Christ, that the name of Christ may be glorified in you and you in Him. Faithful is He that has called you, who also will do it. To Him be glory both now and forever.

Amen.

Finis.

PREFACE *to the* FINAL CHAPTER
That You Might Receive Dr. Increase Mather's Testimony

When the eight sermons on early piety were being delivered, the ministers who preached them waited on the their venerable father, Dr. Increase Mather, with a request that he would permit some discourse of his on that important subject. They wished that his discourse would be ushered in next to theirs. That he might let it fall as a mantle to us, now that God is quickly taking him away from our head. In answer to their desire (though he has already cultivated the subject in several treaties, especially, his Call to the Rising Generation, which have been formerly published, and some of them have had several editions), he preached the short sermon, that is now to fasten the nails that have been set in the preceding essays.

It must be considered that this is a sermon of most uncommon circumstances, being of one who is in the eighty-third year of his age, and who may say, *audite senem juvenes, quem juvenem senes audierunt.*[1] As at this very great age, the servant of God preaches (which he has done all his days) without using any notes, thus also, he does it sometimes almost without writing any. Nor could we have come at this particular sermon if we had not been beholden to the pen of a pious gentlewoman belonging to his flock, who gives us this copy of what the ready-writer took from him, as he delivered it.

The circumstances mentioned, oblige us to conclude that these are some of the last words to be expected from a faithful servant of God, finishing his testimony to those ways of early piety, of which God has made him an eminent instance as well as a renowned preacher. What we have now to wish for the rising generation is that they may receive his testimony, and walk in the good ways of those that have gone before them.

---

1. "Listen, young and old; I heard a young man aged"

ADVICE to the CHILDREN of GODLY ANCESTORS

Dr. Increase Mather, Boston, July 1721

1 Samuel 8:5
They said unto Samuel, "Your sons do not walk in your ways."

We have, in this chapter, the children of Israel weary of the theocracy, which they had been under a long time and asking for a king after the manner of the nations. The reason they give for it is that the sons of Samuel did not walk in his ways. Samuel had grown aged and made use of his own sons for his assistance in the government, hoping that they would walk in his ways, but they did otherwise. Therefore, the elders of Israel came in a whole body to Samuel and complained to him of the ill government of his family.

It is a sad observation, which we have now before us that the sons of good men do not always walk in the good ways which their fathers have walked in. We will consider this doctrine in several propositions.

Proposition I: *All good men do walk in the same way.*

It is that which is called the *"way of good men."* *"Walk in the way of goodness, and keep to the paths of righteousness"* (Prov. 2:20). It is also called the *"old paths"* and the *"good way"* (Jer. 6:16.) It is likewise called *"the way everlasting"* (Ps. 139:24.). From the beginning of the world, good men have always chosen to walk in that way, that way of truth, laying the judgments of God before them.

Particularly, first, it is the way of piety. They have always, like Samuel, worshipped God and Him only, and have been careful not to take the name of God in vain, and have sanctified the Holy Sabbaths of God. Sanctifying the Sabbath is indeed so great a part of piety that it is a part of all godliness (Isa. 58:13).

Secondly, it is the way of righteousness. They are conscientiously careful to observe the first table of the moral law, and of the second table also. Therefore, Paul could say, *"I myself always strive to have a conscience without offense toward God and men"* (Acts 24:16). Thus it was with Samuel. He was upright. He could appeal to the people as in the 12th chapter of this book, *"Whom have I cheated"* (1 Sam. 12:3)? And Israel said, *"You have not cheated us or oppressed us, nor have you taken anything from any man's hand"* (1 Sam. 12:4). But, his sons were very unrighteous. They ran after filthy lucre, they took bribes, and they perverted judgment, which was quite contrary to what their father did.

Thirdly, it is the way of prayerfulness. Thus Samuel said to the people, *"Far be it from me that I should sin against the Lord in ceasing to pray for you"* (1 Sam. 12:23). Good men are praying men. This is *"the generation of those who seek Him"* (Ps. 24:6). They that seek the face of God are the generation that belong to Him. There is not even one godly man in all the world who is not a praying man. *"For this cause everyone who is godly shall pray to You"* (Ps. 32:6). As for those that are prayerless, they are mentioned among the *"workers of iniquity"* (Ps. 14:4). If they are prayerless, they are so to be accounted. Thus we see in short, the good ways, that good men are forever found walking in, the ways of a Samuel!

Proposition II: *The children of godly men have peculiar advantages to serve the God of their fathers, and walk in the good ways which their fathers walked in, various advantages which other children in the world have not.*

First, they have the Scriptures. They have the Word of God to direct them in the way of life and salvation. As is said concerning the Jews, *"What advantage then has the Jew, or what is the profit of circumcision? Much in every way! Chiefly because to them were committed the oracles of God"* (Rom. 3:1-2). They had the Holy Scriptures. Thus, it was said of how Timothy was advantaged in that respect above others. *"From childhood you have known the Holy Scriptures, which are able to make you wise for salvation"* (2 Tim. 3:15).

They have also the word of God preached unto them, as the written Word of God. Likewise the gospel being preached unto them is a great advantage. The preaching of the gospel is the ordinary means by which true faith in the Lord Jesus Christ is wrought in the souls of His elect. *"Faith comes by hearing, and hearing by the word of God"* (Rom. 10:17). In that regard, the children of godly men have special advantages to know the God of their fathers.

Secondly, they are the subjects of parental instructions, and they are taught by their parents how they ought to serve God. Thus the Lord required His people of old to teach His commandments *"diligently to your children"* (Deut. 6:7).

"For He established a testimony in Jacob, and appointed a law in Israel, which He commanded our fathers, that they should make them known to their children; That the generation to come might know them, the children who would be born, that they may arise and declare them to their children" (Ps. 78:5-6).

And the Lord said concerning Abraham, *"I know Abraham, 'that he may command his children and his household after him, that they keep the way of the Lord'"* (Gen. 18:19).

Now, they that are the children of Abraham will do the works of Abraham. So we find that the servants of God have always done this. David taught his son Solomon and his other children. He said, *"Come, you children, listen to me; I will teach you the fear of the Lord"* (Ps. 34:11). And his son Solomon says, *"When I was my father's son, tender and the only one in the sight of my mother, he also taught me"* (Prov. 4:3-4). So did his godly mother also carefully instruct him. We read how his godly mother instructed him, saying, *"What, my son? And what, son of my womb? And what, son of my vows?"* (Prov. 31:2) Will you not hear the counsel of her that has so often prayed for you and vowed and offered many sacrifices to God on your behalf?

Thirdly, the people of God put up many prayers for their children that God would give them His grace. They pray, *"Give my son Solomon a loyal heart"* (1 Chron. 29:19). Thus Abraham prayed for Ishmael, and God said, concerning Ishmael, *"I have heard you"* (Gen. 17:20). Their advantages are peculiar in that respect, in that they are prayed for.

Lastly, they have the blessing of their parents, which is not a light thing. The blessing of a father is not to be despised, rather, it ought to be regarded. We see Esau as bad as he was, yet when he saw he was deprived of his father's blessing, he wept and made a great and bitter cry upon it. Verily, it is a considerable, a valuable thing for children to have their pious parents' imploring and pronouncing of blessings upon them in the name of the Lord. So, the children of Godly parents have advantages which other children in the world are strangers to.

Proposition III: *Many children of godly parents, do prove godly too, and walk in the good ways of their parents, yet it is too often sadly otherwise.*

Some will observe that God has so cast the line of election that, for the most part, it runs through the loins of godly parents. The second epistle of John is *"To the elect lady and her children"* (2 John 1). If the mother is elected, there is more hope and encouragement that the children belong to the election too.

We read, *"The mercy of the Lord is from everlasting to everlasting on those who fear Him, and His righteousness to children's children"* (Ps. 103:17).

Thus, Paul says concerning Timothy, in 2 Timothy 1:5, that *"I am persuaded [this genuine faith] is in you also"* that you are a true believer, when I call to remembrance the faith that was in thy grandmother Lois, and thy mother Eunice. Your grandmother was a godly woman, your mother a holy woman; therefore I cannot but hope the more for you. Doubtless, if an account of it were taken, it would be found that the greatest part of those who belong to God have descended from godly parents.

Proposition IV: *But still, the grace of God is sovereign. It is not engaged to any particular family.*

He is free in the disposing of His grace. He says, *"I will be gracious to whom I will be gracious, and I will have compassion on whom I will have compassion"* (Ex. 33:19). The fact that so many children that descend from godly parents are not godly themselves is a sad truth. I will first show the proof of it, then inquire whence it comes to pass. For the proof of it:

We find in the Scripture that many particular families did degenerate from the faith of their forefathers. Let us look back as far as Adam's family, and we will find it so. Adam had a godly son whose name was Seth. Now the posterity of that godly son, in process of time, did degenerate and became as the rest of the world, *"The sons of God saw the daughters of men"* (Gen. 6:2). The sons of God, that is to say the posterity of godly Seth, degenerated and became like the rest of the world.

Noah had a godly son, Shem, but this man's posterity did sadly degenerate. Note that they became idolaters (Josh. 24:2). In Abraham's family, there was Ishmael that would scoff at his brother, who was a godly man. In Isaac's family Esau was a profane person. So says the apostle, *"Take heed 'lest there be any fornicator or profane person like Esau, who for one morsel of food sold his birthright'"* (Heb. 12:15-16). In David's family, how many wicked sons sprung up in that good man's family! Amnon, who committed incest with his own sister, Absalom that murdered his brother Amnon, and after that would have murdered his own father to have gained the kingdom!

Is it not said of Nabal, who was a drunkard, that *"he was of the house of Caleb"* (1 Sam. 25:3)? A sad thing that so vile a wretch as Nabal should descend from such a house as Caleb's was! Josiah was a godly man, yet his children were all bad! God said to one of these, *"Did not your father ... do justice and righteousness"* (Jer. 22:15)? *"Yet your eyes and your heart are for nothing but your covetousness, for shedding innocent blood, and practicing oppression and violence"* (Jer. 22:16-17).

Apostate Nations

The same is true concerning whole generations. Sometimes whole generations have apostatized from God and become exceedingly sinful in His sight, as when Joshua was dead it is said, *"Another generation arose after them who did not know the Lord nor the work which He had done for Israel"* (Judg. 2:10). A whole generation did degenerate from the piety of their fathers that had gone before them. *"Yet I had planted you a noble vine, a seed of highest quality. How then have you turned before Me into the degenerate plant of an alien vine?"* (Jer. 2:25).

Ungodly Children

Secondly, how is it that godly men sometimes have very ungodly children! To answer this question, first, the children of godly men are born as sinful as the children of other men. They have original corruption in them as much as others have. Hence, David says, *"Behold, I was brought forth in iniquity, and in sin my mother conceived me"* (Ps. 51:5). Yet David's mother was a singular good woman, a very holy woman. David, when He prayed to God, says, *"Oh, turn to me, and have mercy on me! Give Your strength to Your servant, and save the son of Your maidservant"* (Ps. 86:16).

His father Jesse was also a very holy man. The Jews call him *"Jesse the righteous,"* and have such an opinion of him, that they hyperbolically say, *"The angel of death could find no sin but that of our first parents, to charge him with."* David was the son of a godly father and a godly mother, yet he was conceived in sin and shaped in iniquity. Such are as apt to sin as the children of ungodly men. They are apt to tell lies as soon as they are born. When they commit a fault, they are apt to tell a lie, because of the corruption which is natural to them. Yea, they are *"inventors of evil things"* (Rom. 1:30). They are apt to commit such sins as never any did before them. They are apt to do amiss and to fall in with the ways of sin.

Corrupt Churches

Thirdly, this comes to pass from the malice of Satan, who does what he can to corrupt the churches. Among the wheat, there springs up a world of tares. How comes this to pass? Why says the text, *"an enemy has done this"* (Matt. 13:28). The Devil is that enemy. The Devil is an enemy to purity in churches. He would have churches to be like the rest of the world, therefore, he sows tares in the Lord's field. He does it, in the degeneracy that he labors to introduce among the children of the covenant.

Death of Godly Men

Fourthly, it comes to pass from the removal of eminent servants of God. Thus Paul, when going from Ephesus, says, *"After my departure savage wolves will come in among you"* (Acts 20:29). How often is it said in the book of Judges, while the good judges continued, things went well, but when those good judges were dead and removed out of the way, the people presently degenerated and became like the rest of the world, and became guilty of such sins as others in the world were guilty of. Thus, we see the doctrine cleared in the particulars that have been mentioned.

Application

I. Hence, we see that men ought not to set their hearts inordinately upon their children.

Indeed, they are apt to promise themselves much comfort in their children. We see it as Abraham says, *"Lord God, what will You give me, seeing I go childless"* (Gen. 15:2)? It is threatened as a judgment, such a man will die childless. We see it in Rachel, *"Give me children, or else I die"* (Gen. 30:1). God gave her children, and she died for it, and when her soul was departing, she called His name Benoni, that is, *"the child of my affliction."*

Parents who know not how their children may prove, should not set their hearts inordinately upon their children. Who knows, but that child that you are so fond of may prove to you as Esau did to Rebecca and his father? He was a grief of mind to them both. And Rebecca said, *"I am weary of my life because of the daughters of Heth"* (Gen. 27:46).

II. If the children of good men may prove ungodly, it is no wonder the children of ungodly men do so.

Children are more apt to imitate their parents in that which is evil, than in that which is good. *"The children gather wood, the fathers kindle the fire, and the women knead dough, to make cakes for the queen of heaven"* (Jer. 7:18). Abominable! To make cakes to the queen of heaven, to worship the moon!

Yet, when the parents did so, the children did so too, and it is no wonder they did. The Samaritans that succeeded those that were carried captive worshipped graven images and served other gods. *"So these nations feared the Lord, yet served their carved images; also their children and their children's children have continued doing as their fathers did, even to this day"* (2 Kings 17:41). Those children that did mock the holy prophet Elisha who said, *"Go up, you baldhead! Go up, you baldhead"* (2 Kings 2:23). You say your master Elijah has gone up to heaven. Would these children have done so, if they had not seen the iniquity of their fathers? Doubtless their fathers were guilty of the same iniquity.

III. We may see by this, that it is not in the power of parents to give grace to their children.

They may give them what they have of this world, but that is all. To have grace given to them, it is a thousand times better, far more desirable than to have a portion of this world's goods. But this is more than they can give. They cannot give them sanctifying grace. Parents cannot give them true repentance. That is the gift of God, not of their parents. They cannot give them faith in Jesus Christ. None but God can give this. A godly man can no more make his children godly than he can raise the dead out of their graves. None but God can do it, and He alone must have the praise and glory of it.

IV. It is not safe for children to build upon having Abraham for their father.

"Do not think to say to yourselves, 'We have Abraham as our father'" (Matt. 3:9). This is a foundation not to be built upon. You may have a father as good a man as Abraham, and yet perish forever in your unbelief. How was it with one who died and went to hell, and when in torments there he cried out, *"Father Abraham have mercy on me"* (Luke 16:24)! This child of Abraham, in torment, adds, *"I have five brothers, that he [Abraham] may testify to them, lest they also come to this place of torment"* (Luke 16:28).

Why? Is there any charity in hell? No, but they know if their brethren come there it would be worse for them, an aggravation of their misery! Well then, you that are the children of godly parents, I will speak a solemn word unto you. If you live and die in your impenitence, you will have the most terrible witnesses against you. Your father and your mother that loved you so dearly, that have wept and prayed for you so many times, your father and your mother, they will condemn you, they will justify God in His condemning of you. They will join with the Lord in passing a sentence of eternal condemnation upon you at the last day, and say like the angel in the Revelations, *"You are righteous, O Lord, the One who is and who was and who is to be, because You have judged these things"* (Rev. 16:5). Thus, it will be said at the last day. Your father and your mother will say *"Lord I concur with You; You are righteous in passing a sentence of* eternal condemnation upon this child of mine. I warned him many a time to repent and turn to God, but he would not, so that You are righteous in all that has come upon him."

V. The children of Godly men should be careful that they themselves are godly.

Now the children of New England are (or once were), for the most part, the children of godly men. What did our fathers come into this wilderness for? Not to gain estates, as men do now, but for religion, and that they might lead their children in a hopeful way of being truly religious. There was a famous man that preached before one of the greatest assemblies that ever was preached unto, seventy years ago, and he told them, *"I have lived in a country seven years, and all that time I never heard one profane oath, and all that time I never did see a man drunk in that land."*

Where was that country? It was New England! New England! New England! But, ah, degenerate New England, what have you come to at this day? How those sins have become common in you, that once were not so much as heard of in this land? A sad thing it is! Well then, oh turn to God, you that are children of godly parents. Remember that God calls you to it. Now, He calls you to it in a solemn way by a grievous disease He has sent into this town, which, how far it may proceed, we know not. Is not God speaking to you now? It will be a wonder in that the slain of the disease are not very many before this disease be over. Children, you are concerned to turn to God, to make sure of Christ. Then you will be happy. Nothing else can make you happy. You cannot be sure of your lives. You may make sure of Christ. If you make sure of Him, you will be happy whatever befalls you.

Well, what will we do to make sure of this? A few solemn words I wish to speak to you, and so I leave you.

Seek God early.

You read, *"Those who seek me diligently will find me"* (Prov. 8:17). O, that there may be many early seekers of God, many that set themselves in good earnest to seek Him. Remember the solemn exhortation that David gave to his son Solomon:

"As for you, my son Solomon, know the God of your father, and serve Him with a loyal heart and with a willing mind; for the Lord searches all hearts and understands all the intent of the thoughts. If you seek Him, He will be found by you; but if you forsake Him, He will cast you off forever" (1 Chron. 28:9).

Say not, *"We cannot convert ourselves."* True, but do not do that which will hinder your conversion. Do not hearken to evil counsel. We read that Ahaziah, after the death of his father, the house of Ahab was *"his counselors after the death of his father, to his destruction"* (2 Chron. 22:4). Remember that Scripture, *"He who walks with wise men will be wise, but the companion of fools will be destroyed"* (Prov. 13:20). O, let not any of you be a companion of such. If you love your souls, beware of vain company, for there is nothing more destructive to the souls of men than that. If you choose to follow them, they will be your ruin, and they will undo you forever.

Wait on God in the use of His own means, that He would be merciful to you.

Therefore, give diligent attention, even an earnest heed unto the Word of God, when it is preached unto you. Do not set yourselves to sleep at sermons. I remember, there was a man who died in this place many years ago, who died in doleful despair. This man, when dying, said to me, *"Sometimes I set myself to sleep on purpose when you have been preaching, and do you think there is any mercy for me?"*

Yes, there was mercy for him if he repented, but he died in doleful despair. Take heed of setting yourselves to sleep, when you should be hearing as for your lives, as for your souls. Then also, cry to God that He would have mercy on you. Do as Paul, when in the pangs of the new birth it is said of him, *"Behold he prays!"* Doubtless Saul prayed many times before that. He was a Pharisee. The Pharisees often prayed, but he did not pray in earnest. Now, he prayed in good earnest, as if his soul was concerned, as indeed it was. Pray as such for your life and soul, and God will hear and answer you.

Lastly, do not quench the Spirit of God. It is complained of the Jews, *"You always resist the Holy Spirit"* (Acts 7:51). That is a dangerous thing, to vex the Spirit of God, to grieve the Spirit of God! God has said, *"My Spirit shall not strive with man forever"* (Gen. 6:3). Dr. Preston speaks of a man, that had been guilty of a great sin, and was troubled very much that he had been guilty of such a sin. He went to a vile companion that gave him this wicked advice, such that Satan himself could not have given him worse. *"Go thy way, commit that sin again, and you shall be never troubled more."* That poor wretch did so, and he was never troubled more.

God gave him up to a reprobate mind, to hardness of heart. Remember Saul. It is said, *"The Spirit of the Lord departed from Saul"* (1 Sam. 16:14). And, *"Woe to them when I depart from them"* (Hosea 9:12)! If you sin against the strivings of God's Spirit, you may provoke Him utterly to depart from you. Woe unto you! Think of an awful Scripture which I will leave with you, for

I knew a man many years ago whose conversion to God was promoted by serious meditation on that very Scripture. *"Because I have cleansed you, and you were not cleansed, you will not be cleansed of your filthiness anymore, till I have caused My fury to rest upon you"* (Ezek. 24:13).

Now, may the God of our fathers mercifully preserve the children of New England from that apostasy which may provoke Him to cast them off forever. May He be with them, as He was with their fathers, and help them to walk in the good ways of their fathers, in that faith and order of the gospel which they walked in, and may He never leave them nor forsake them.

THE END.